Ron Hopwood
55 Sherwood Avenue
Walderslade, Chatham
Kent ME5 9PP
Telephone - 01634 201165

CW00552381

What Do They Want?

HARVARD UNIVERSITY

The President and Fellows
of Harvard College present
this certificate to

Sammy Price

in grateful recognition of his service as
Visiting Artist during 1984–85
and of his contribution to the Arts.
*Given at Cambridge, Massachusetts in
the Year of Our Lord, nineteen hundred
and eighty-five and of Harvard College
the three hundred and forty-ninth.*

PRESIDENT

SECRETARY

WHAT DO THEY WANT?
A Jazz Autobiography

by

SAMMY PRICE

Edited by

Caroline Richmond

Chronological discography

compiled by

Bob Weir

Bayou Press

First published in the United Kingdom 1989 by
Bayou Press Limited
117 High Street
Wheatley, Oxford

British Library Cataloguing in Publication Data
Price, Sammy, 1908–
    What do they want: a jazz autobiography.
    1. Jazz — biographies
    I. Title II. Richmond, Caroline, 1951–
    785.42'092'4

ISBN 1-871478–25–1

Contents

Editor's Note and Acknowledgements

Sammy Price has been working towards publishing his autobiography for many years. It is, for example, almost exactly two decades since Max Jones mentioned it in an interview with Sammy in the *Melody Maker* ('Call it Sam's Song,' 20 December 1969), and the author has frequently alluded to its forthcoming appearance during the intervening period. Here at last is 'Sam's Song.'

When I first met Sammy, towards the end of 1986, a large table in his apartment on Fifth Avenue in New York held several piles of autobiographical papers and a large number of fascinating photographs. I began work on the lengthy task of bringing the material together and placing the various drafts of Sammy's life story in chronological order. By early 1987, however, it was becoming clear that while some episodes in his career were exhaustively covered, elsewhere there were definite 'gaps.' In order to bridge some of these gaps, Alyn Shipton taped several conversations with Sammy during a visit to New York in 1987. Once transcribed, these passages were slotted into their appropriate places and the narrative approved by the author. We also asked Sammy to write a final section describing a few of his more recent activities, and he duly obliged with 'The Life and Times of Sammy Price in Boston,' which is incorporated in the last chapter. While the final version of his story has been drawn from various sources, reflecting perhaps the long gestation of the book, the voice that tells it is Sammy's alone.

I feel extremely privileged to have met Sammy, to have been treated to his generous hospitality, to have heard him play, and to have been instrumental in helping his memoirs finally reach publication. My thanks go to him for remaining patient during the last couple of years and for keeping faith that publication would indeed eventually take place. In this I am first and foremost indebted to Alyn Shipton, who was initially responsible for transmitting to me his enthusiasm for working with jazz musicians on their autobiographies, and without whom none of my work would have been possible. I am grateful to both Dan Kochakian and Paul Oliver, who provided further source material, and to Bob Weir, who has willingly revised his discography on a number of occasions to take account of research carried out by many of his collegues; early drafts were an invaluable aid to chronology during editorial work.

The plate sections consist of photographs drawn from Sammy Price's collection, and are reproduced by permission. The author gratefully acknowledges prints made available by Dan Kochakian; Adamsfotos, Miami; Parris Photo Studio, Philadelphia; Nicholas Alexaki; Studio Chadel, Nice; R. C. Hickman; Rock-Ola, Antwerp; Jean-Pierre Leloir; Roger Pariente; Raymond Ross; Claude Mitchell; Bernard Amiard; Studio One, New York; Nancy Miller Elliott; and Howard O. Allen.

Caroline Richmond
April, 1989

1

From Honey Grove to Waco

I did not ask to come into this world on 6 October 1908, and, on many occasions, I've been sorry it happened. It all got started in Honey Grove, a small town in east Texas, where the slogan was written in big bold letters, "the blackest land and the whitest people." This slogan was meant for white people, and at an early age I used to hear people say, "Nigger, do not let the sun go down on you here."

"Nigger" was the word most heard in my neighborhood. In the early 1900s, like now, black people called each other "nigger" with affection. Back then, like now, white folks said it with a lot of hate. The difference was that then "nigger" was your only name, and you could be damn sure that if you did anything other than shut up, bow your head and take it, it was only a matter of hours before you were just another of who knows how many dead niggers.

It was early morning when my grandmother told the big kids to light the fire under the big pot because she thought my mother, Alberta, one of the 14 kids that she and my grandfather had, would need it. The big black kettle was like the center of my family's day-to-day existence. My grandmother was in charge of that big pot, my mother second in command. Every now and then one of the big kids got to light the kindling under the pot to heat water for cooking, washing clothes, hog killing or, most importantly, taking a bath. What the older boys did was to stack five rows of bricks in a round circle three bricks high, and make a fire under the big pot right in the center. Like clockwork and before the sun set in the west, I was here on planet earth.

My father and mother lived with my grandparents and moved every year because my grandfather was an AME minister. When they had a quarterly conference, which was a meeting of the various church flocks, their leaders would come together and there would be a presiding bishop who would determine where the assignments would be. Well, in ten years my grandfather had an assignment in ten different cities. He wondered why. What he would do was go into a town where the conditions were deplorable and there were inadequate facilities for the church meetings, and he would take his 14 children, his grandchildren and his in-laws with him and build a new church. Finally he asked the presiding elder why it was that he was always moved. "Well," said the elder, "can't you see the handwriting on the wall? When you go into a new city and build a church each year, everybody want you. You have to go to cities where the conditions are deplorable and the people poor, because the Church plays an important role in keeping niggers in their places." You see, they had to have a liaison person between the white man and the Blacks, and, quite naturally, this was usually the minister. So that was the history of doing quite a bit of traveling on my grandfather's part for the first ten years of my life.

My father wanted to get out from under that condition, but I think he was afraid of my mother's 13 brothers and sisters. Whenever he would talk about moving, they would take care of his suitcase, so he would just lie low. He couldn't win – there were too many of them. My grandfather was a good man, but I never heard of him act as a peacemaker in these affairs.

Getting back to the big pot, maybe when I was born I should have jumped into the fire, and then I would not have to review the last 70 years of my life. I lived through two world wars, the Vietnam affair, the sinking of the Titanic, the loss of Amelia Earhart, and Lindbergh crossing the Atlantic alone. I lived through the various amendments to the constitution, which gave us certain rights that I thought would never come to pass, such as the School Rights Bill, the right to vote, and better conditions in the South as well as the North. When I was a kid I thought the rules were made by the Klu Klux Klan. When they told all niggers to get off the street they meant it, and the following day usually found a dead nigger. Black people had no rights, and that was that.

If a black kid did something wrong in Texas, they'd keep him until he's 21, and a lot of kids knew it. So sometimes when a black kid became involved in some wrongdoing, he just went to the limit, 'cause he knew what to expect anyway. The reform school in Texas was called Gatesville, and the stories that used to come out of Gatesville were stories of brutality that you never heard of. And so it was dangerous in a sense: you couldn't be out late at night, you couldn't go certain places, you had to use the back door when you entered a business or a home, and a thousand and one other things. But if you were wise, if you were smart, and not negligent, you could survive. That's the way it was.

In any place that there were white people you had to take your hat off and say, "Yessir," "No, sir," "Thank you, missy," and "Please," and you had to be very humble. So what I did when I was 14 or 15, I got a divorce from my hat, and I made this divorce stick for almost 50 years. I figured there was no point in having to tip my hat or take my hat off to anybody, so I just threw the damn thing away. That eliminated part of that problem. Although from time to time since then I've worn hats, it wasn't under the conditions where I had to be humble. And I'm courteous anyway. I probably would just tip my hat to a person and take my hat off as a matter of courtesy, because I feel within that that's the feeling that a person should have if they have your respect.

After living with my grandparents for two years my Daddy finally gathered enough nerve to go out on his own. We moved from Honey Grove to Greenville, where my mother got a job as a housekeeper for a white family who gave us a two-room shack at the rear of their big white house. This accommodation for live-in servants was common in those days. It was a little better because we didn't have to line up to go to the bathroom, and that included ladies and babies. One memory of this two-room shack in Greenville is the story my mother used to tell about the time my brother, Robert, set the house on fire. I was about two years old and could not walk (I was almost three before I learned, but after I got the hang of it I walked up a breeze), and my brother was about four years old. Robert was playing with matches and started a fire in the bed. He ran up to the big white house and told my mother that she had better come out to the little house because Bubba, meaning me, was in trouble. My mother rushed out to the house and there I was sitting up in the bed laughing while smoke was everywhere. My mother got me out of the bed and gave Robert a backhand lick in the face, although he hollered that he didn't do it.

The very next day my father went off and found work at the Braxos Bakery in Waco. This job paid $6 a week, more money than Daddy had ever heard of. Plans were made to leave Greenville and join my father, who went on ahead to get things set up for us. When the day came to catch the train, we were up at 4.00 a.m. There was glee and happiness everywhere because this meant that, for the very first time, we would have our own house.

We were met at the station by my father with a horse and wagon. He took us to a two-room house in West Station, just outside of East Waco. It was a cute house with a garden in the front and back, and we fell in love with our new home. The following day my father went off to work and a stranger came to the screen door dressed in heavy make-up and feathers and carrying an umbrella. Back then, no matter how strange, you went right ahead and let people in, which is exactly what my mother did. As soon as this odd character was in he started chasing after me, then my mother and my brother. It was probably quite a sight, this guy in feathers and all, who I'm told was a fortune teller, and the three of us running all around our little shack. It was all pretty uneventful in the end. Our neighbor heard the commotion and came over and kicked the feathered crazy out. Once he was gone we spent hours having a big laugh over the whole thing.

After a few months my mother wanted to move to Waco because, by this time, her sister Virginia had married a man by the name of Mr John Henderson, and had moved to Paul Quinn Street in Waco. My brother was to enter school and my father gave in to my mother and got a house for us in Waco out on the Corsicana Road. I was about four then. So my father was no longer a squatter with my grandmother and grandfather, but the worm had turned and he had been invaded by my grandmother and grandfather, my uncles, aunts, and cousins. It was almost like being in Honey Grove; the only difference was that my father was paying the bills, while before he was one of the freeloaders.

To mention Waco was like talking about Heaven. Now, I'll tell you something, and this is a fact: do you know I was 30 years of age, and getting around in fast circles, before I realized that Jerusalem was not in Heaven. All that the Church used to teach about going into Beulah Land, crossing the River Jordan, and walking into Jerusalem just like John, I thought that meant I had to die and go to Heaven. And I was almost 30 before I knew that if I wanted to go to Jerusalem all I would have to do is buy a ticket and get on an airplane or boat.

As far as I was concerned, going to Waco I was going to the biggest city on earth. I mean, I thought that if it rained in Waco, it rained in the next county, the next state; it rained in New York, Chicago and Washington, those places I'd heard of that I figured were just about the same – though not as important – as Waco. I'm not lying when I tell you I truly believed that when it rained in Waco it rained all over the world.

In a way, moving to Waco was the start of my life as a musician. Being raised in a family of religious preachers and gospel singers, the music I had heard was lullabies and church songs. I hadn't any musical instruction, so at that point in my life music was the farthest thing from my mind. But Waco was where I got hooked on it, learned how to play the piano, stood up and performed in front of crowds, met the people whose encouragement I'll always remember and be grateful for. It's not just some vague personal sensation I have about becoming a musician in Waco, 'cause that's where it happened. I came into that town with about as much interest in music as any other little kid, and I left it loving music.

We lived about two blocks from my aunt and used to visit

her all the time. She worked for a doctor who had given her a piano to get it out of the way. This was no ordinary piano, it was a ten-foot grand. I do not know why my aunt took the piano, but she was just like a gypsy and would take anything that people would give her. The thing I forgot to tell you was that she had only two rooms, and I have always tried to figure out how she fit that big piano into a room. It was just like trying to figure out how the Pyramids were built. I was sure they put the piano in a spot and then built the room around it. For the first time in my life I saw someone play the piano. As a small child I had no idea that some day I would be able to master this monster and bring it under my command.

Even though my grandfather was a minister, I wasn't really old enough to go to church until we were living in Waco. Part of surviving life in a white man's world was showing that you were a good Christian, and that meant going to church every Sunday. As a matter of fact, Sunday was nothing but church all day long. First there was Sunday school, then everyone gathered for the main service at about 11 in the morning. In the afternoon there were usually some special singers that would do their thing. After that there was night service. When that was over there wasn't much left to do more than go home and call it a day.

Black services were almost all music and singing. There was a lot of singing. Seeing as there weren't any white people around to intimidate anybody, everybody really sang hard. It was almost in a way like a party for black folk: you got together, dressed up, socialized and had a pretty good time singing and hearing music.

There's some misinformation about black music during those days that I'd like to set straight here and now. A lot of people talk abut how many great black piano players there were in that part of the country that got going playing piano at church services. I didn't see that many pianos. Some time I would like to go to Wurlitzer's and look in the archives and see how many pianos were sold in various regions, and I'd bet it would be alarming and shocking that there were a very few. Sometimes you saw an organ – not an organ like you see in churches now, but a little one that you played with your foot. The real instruments were the human voice and human hands. That was enough for me, though. I loved to go to church and I always made sure I went to every little religious gathering I could just so as I could be around music.

Another thing about instruments, just about the only instruments that Blacks had any access to, could get their hands on or make, were percussion instruments: an occasional drum, tambourines, the triangle. And then there was the harmonica, and sometimes someone had a guitar, but that's about it. The only other instruments I knew about were the violin and the cornet. The violin was for white folks. We had a few cornets, but they were so rare that it wasn't worth mentioning. There were very few marching bands that I can recall. People usually marched with drums. Well, before I left Waco they did have some marching bands, but around 1912, 1913, there were very few. There was also this war hysteria, that was just before World War I, when in 1914 you had the conflict in Europe. People marched, but they didn't march with bands.

You know, all these people talk about who did this and that back then. Well, I was there, and I'll tell you all the black music that was supposed to be happening, all the musicians that were supposed to be playing in churches and on the street and in clubs and all, weren't – not then. The simple reason was that black folk couldn't get their hands on any instruments, and those that did played church music. The Blacks that played something other than church music were very rare and in a way considered sort of dangerous, vulgar. There was Eubie Blake, of course, and a few others like him, but the piano wasn't in tune because they didn't have that many piano tuners. And maybe Buddy Bolden and Bunk Johnson were playing then, but that was in New Orleans, and they were about ten years ahead of their time. Jazz and blues were played by outlaws in dives and at juke joints, '49 camps and picnics. Black people scorned any music that wasn't church music because the structure of black families was very religious at that time. To sing songs about drinking and women and day-to-day life was considered deviant; it led to trouble in the white man's world.

In 1913 my brother went off to school. The next year I got a job shining shoes and made a little money, and then a year after that I walked that long mile down the Corsicana Road to East Waco Elementary School on Paul Quinn Street, where I entered the first grade. This was the year after Germany started World War I. The United States didn't get into the war until 1917. I used to sit around the square and the shoeshine parlors in Waco then and hear the soldiers from England, who were being trained as air pilots, tell of the many events in their far-off country. I got a big kick out of this kind of conversation.

When I was seven years old, I remember going to see some of my mother's friends in another part of town. When me, my mother and brother got on the streetcar, we had to pay our fares in the front and walk the length of the car to sit in the colored section. On that particular day there were some football players from Baylor University sitting in the white section and they started a big fight with us. They tripped us up and punched my mother. My mother didn't take no shit from nobody, and when they said, fight, she was ready. So were we. We jumped up, and there was a sign setting on an angle saying "Colored" on one side, "White" on the other. I jumped up and got that sign, and boy, I was beating those guys. I think they thought it would be just a little mêlée where "These niggers are going to run," and all that. But, boy, we fought 'em. The streetcar man was flabbergasted on seeing this and he drove as fast as he could to the center of town to get help. Well, the outcome was that the police let all of the white guys go, but I'm sure they always remembered that little old colored woman and her two boys on that day.

My mother and father used to take us to the fairs and carnivals in Waco, and it was at that time that I noticed the drums and cornet, and decided that I would learn to play both of them. I learned about a man named Professor Cobb who taught the cornet for 25 cents a lesson, and I asked my mother if I could take lessons from him. She was very willing to pay for the lessons, probably because I was beginning to show some signs, along with my brother Robert, of developing skills as the world's youngest hustler, and she was happy to pay for something that might lead to a legitimate life style. It took only two weeks for Professor Cobb to give up on me. "Mrs Price," he said to my mother, "your son ain't got it. He just doesn't have it. He don't understand what it's all about."

I guess my mother wanted to know what the hell "it" was, and replied, "Well, do you think he can learn?" Well, I guess the cornet just wasn't my instrument, because 25 cents a week wasn't even worth it to Professor Cobb. He laid it on the line. "He can never learn," he said. "He has no concept of tonal qualities, and that's that. Save your 25 cents." I couldn't understand how this man could look into my inner self and tell me what was inside, and besides, all I ever saw him do was look into the mirror at his mustache – you know, the handlebar kind that stood up at the end. This discouragement has been, up until today, a stumbling block in my musical career. What I am trying to explain is that his evaluation of my musical capabilities affected my ability to learn rudimentary elements in music.

Being a child, I was hurt to have him say this to my mother, but I didn't let it stop me. I went to every kind of show that came to Waco. We had a keen interest in the carnivals and the medicine and vaudeville shows. In most of the cases there would be a blues singer in the show. There was a little theater on Bridge Street, called the Gaiety Theater, where they used to have vaudeville shows from time to time. One time we got permission from my mother to go there. We had to cross the Brazos River to get to the theater, and my mother told us to hold onto our hats while crossing the bridge, as it was quite windy that day. My brother was so excited about seeing the show that when we came to the middle of the bridge he had his hands in his pockets instead of on his hat, and the wind blew his hat into the river.

Anyway, I always sat in the first row as long as the people

in the theater would let me stay. That was my first introduction to a person on the stage. The Gaiety Theater was also a movie theater. You had a choice to go to the Jim Crow nickelodeon theater or to your own theater, where you could sit where you liked. I had an opportunity to see Daybreak Nelson, who was a comedian, Ozzie McPherson, and many dancers and singers of that period.

I was hearing more music, different instruments. For some reason people were getting into different styles of music. Lodges and various organizations would have other instruments. They started developing bands. In the brass bands we had all kinds of instruments for conventions, parades, picnics and occasions like that. Of course they didn't have all these contraptions, all this new stuff. There were marching bands with the big bass drums with the cymbals on top. They played the bass drum with a mallet. Right behind the bass drum would be some guy hitting the snare drum. The drums hit that beat that you felt right through the ground. It was a powerful and moving sound, made to make you feel safe and strong.

By the time I was eight, only a year from Professor Cobb's bad judgement about what I did or didn't have, it seemed to me that there was music all over the place. In 1916 music got into the streets where a black kid could get close to it. I think to learn something about music, about dancing, you got to be exposed to it. You've got to be up close to it. We hadn't had that opportunity: these things were not accessible to black communities. If it's in a white theater and you just pass by and see, it wouldn't mean anything because of the fact that you didn't have an opportunity to see it, because they didn't allow Blacks in many of those places. But now it was war-time, and I guess people needed to hear and make more music in order to feel better. Carnivals started passing through town, and traveling minstrel shows; black people were starting to listen to the blues. It didn't matter if Professor Cobb thought I didn't have it: whatever it was, I *did* have it. By eight years old I knew I had to get it, have it and do it. There was no way to avoid music.

One night my family went to the fair in Waco and to the Cotton Palace. This was a show all about cotton, and once a year there were all kinds of exhibitions for about 19 days at this big fairground, and people from all over the world came together in competition on who had the biggest steer, the best grade of cotton, and so on. My father had one of the food stands at the fair, and my brother and myself had a chance to visit almost every day. They'd have a rodeo and various shows, and one show was always for the colored people. It was here on that night that I first met Ella B. Moore and her husband Chintz, a comedy and dance team who owned a theater in Dallas and came to Waco with a show for the Cotton Palace. I asked my mother if I could meet Mrs Moore and she said, yes. The first thing I wanted to know was where she lived. Her answer was Dallas, and I wanted to know how far that was from Waco. She said it was about 100 miles from Waco. I told her that someday I would come to Dallas, and when I did I would come to visit with her. I did not realize then that Mrs Moore would play an important part in my going out of the state and later becoming a well-known musician.

We also saw and heard Jessie Aikens, a drummer. He could play the melody of a song on his small drum. I know of only one jazz drummer who could do the same thing, and that was Zutty Singleton. After leaving the fairground my mind was still on those drums, but I couldn't say anything to my mother, remembering what the music teacher had said.

When I was older, I remember, I used to ride a motorcycle at the fairground. At the fair each year they used to have all kinds of amusements, and I used to hang around the motordrome. The people knew me, and they let me start up the motorcycles and warm them up, because the riders wouldn't want to go up on the motordrome with a cold motorcycle. So I would start the motor up and I would sit on the motorcycle, race the motor and keep it warmed up: I thought I was a big shot. And when the guy was ready to ride he'd just push it off the rack and go on up.

So one day the lady asked me just to ride around the

bottom part of the motordrome, on the ground. So I was just riding around very slow and she said, "Go up just a little bit on the rim of that thing." So I went up just a little bit. And she said, "Go up a little higher now." And what happened was I went up a little higher and she was on a motorcycle: she got between me and the floor, and that made me have to go up on the damn thing. Well, I knew the principle of gravity, that if you keep the motor pulling against the gravity you won't fall. So I'm riding like hell, up, and she's down below. And her husband gets on a motorcycle and shoots up above me. That was the most frightenening motorcycle ride I ever had.

I know that I became a feature act at this motordrome, a black kid riding a motor cycle. It looked like a ham sandwich, and I'd always be in the middle. I never went up higher than the middle of that ring. And the way that man shot up past me, that was really the thrilling thing.

To get back to that night at the Cotton Palace, from that night on until the summer of 1918 we just day-dreamed about music, always listening to the blues melodies we heard around us day and night. These songs used to come to us from some of the strangest places, and from the start I loved every one of them. Like religion, the blues was also a part of our people. There were many kinds of blues, just as there were different kinds of popular and classical music. I do not agree with many of the critics who class all blues as the same. I have heard a blues where a person would get a new pair of shoes and a song would be made up about it; or, if you lost a girlfriend or boyfriend, another kind of blues would be written, while still another type of blues is when someone near "goes up the country" (meaning to move to a northern city in the USA), and out would come a set of words with a musical pattern to fit it.

A guitar player came past our house one day, and instead of singing the original words of a blues we knew he made up a set of words to describe a lynching that had taken place in a small community called Robinsonville, near Waco. Every few days there used to be some kind of lynching or a killing which involved black folks. Blacks always used to come out with the short end of the stick, and the only hope for the losers was jail or death – take your choice. The words went something like this:

> "I never have, and I never will,
> pick no more cotton in Robinsonville.
> Tell me how long will I have to wait,
> can I get you now or must I hesitate?"

Many of the famous blues songs were composed about something in particular, whether good or bad, just as the famous songsmiths create songs about "June" and "moon" and a thousand other things which we think are silly, but somehow they become very popular with millions all over the world.

You can be sure that words of songs can have an effect on a person. The words of the *Hesitation Blues* made us realize, for the first time, the dangers for a black man of living in the South, so that all the years we lived in Dallas and other cities in the South our hearts were always filled with the hidden fear that we could very well be the subject for one of those blues songs. During these years I had to realize and pay attention to the warnings that I heard every day: "Do not take everyone to be your friend," and, "Be careful of what you say and who you say it to," all of which made me suspicious of almost everyone around me. That kind of thing was not good for me at such an early age, but, nevertheless, I was confronted with it.

Saturday afternoons usually found us on the city square, which was only three miles away, where the guitar players used to meet and entertain the crowds. These troubadours were popular everywhere they appeared. Some of the players came from as far as Dallas, and one of them was Blind Lemon Jefferson. I can hear it now after more than 60 years, the people urging him on with, "Come on, Lemon, pick that box!" He wore a big gray hat, peg-top pants, a striped shirt with elastic armbands, and bulldog shoes. I have heard some critics say that Blind Lemon was fat and greasy and dirty. Well, maybe we're talking about two different people.

I want to tell you a little story about Blind Lemon. He was a peculiar man. I used to hear the story that during those days he used to have whiskey, bootleg whiskey. That was very important for those guys who sang the blues – they had to have whiskey. Now Blind Lemon Jefferson could leave the whiskey at a certain point in the bottle; he could take his left hand, shake that bottle, and feel where the whiskey stopped. He could go away from home and stay all day, and come back at night and shake the bottle and tell you whether that whiskey was gone.

People used to say that Leadbelly and Josh White used to lead Blind Lemon around. He was an awfully proud man, and I can understand why he froze to death in Chicago. J. Mayo Williams, one of the leading record men – black, that is – in America during the 1920s, 1930s and 1940s, told the story about Lemon's death in Chicago in 1930. Someone was to meet him at the LaSalle Station, and when they didn't meet him he tried to walk from the station to the South Side of Chicago. To me, this doesn't sound like a man who needed to be led around. I'm glad that I was around when Lemon was alive so that I can defend this great American troubadour whose voice used to ring out through the crowd: "Going down to the river, take a rocking chair, going down to the river, take a rocking chair, if the blues overtake me, I will rock away from here." In those days it was not unusual to hear singers sing eight-bar blues, and it was then that the blues started to take root in me.

By the time America entered World War I our parents were officially separated. My father had been crowded out, so he'd got us a bigger house on Paul Quinn Street with three rooms and a big yard. He was not getting along with my mother at all. He was fed up with my mother's nagging and was drinking. One night she threw a lit lamp at him, but it didn't stop him and he kept on hitting the bottle. I often think of the great musicians I knew who couldn't stop drinking and ended up at the wrong end of the line.

Anyway, one day we came home for lunch and noticed that my father had the horse and wagon backed up to the back door and was moving everything out of the house. We asked him what it all meant, and he gave us a dollar apiece and told us to go to the store and get whatever we wanted. We didn't know what to think, so we ran off to the store, and when we came home from school at three o'clock everything was gone. He ran away with everything.

The following Sunday I got my first shock. Whatever it was we were eating for dinner, I liked it and asked for more, but my mother said there wasn't any more. From that day on I vowed that there would always be food in my house, and that is the way it is today. I guess my father was just chicken and couldn't face the music. I had to wonder what my mother would do without the support of my father. So my brother and I got jobs shining shoes for a man called Charlie Toosie. He used to pick us up in the morning when we didn't have school. This money was a big help for our little household.

My mother had been thinking about the welfare of me and my brother Robert. It was decided in the spring of 1918 that she would go to Dallas in May and get a job, and that in time she would send for us. The letter came for us to leave Waco on 3rd June, just 16 days before the Emancipation Proclamation, which is celebrated in Texas on 19th June. The ride to Dallas took about three hours on the Inter-urban. This was a kind of oversized streetcar, but smaller than a regular train coach. It was a real thrill for us to have a chance to travel without our parents, and it made us feel like grown persons. We were met at the station by my mother and went to our little house on Cochran Street.

When we arrived in Dallas the first thing I wanted to do was to go down to see the famous Central Tracks where Ella B. Moore's Park Theater was located. It was very easy to get there. You see, all over the South during that period, black people lived in black neighborhoods, so the Central Tracks which ran north and south were easy for me to find. I went to the theater and just stood there for almost an hour, looking at the people and wanting to join the crowd. I was a big boy for my ten years and could very easily have been taken for a teenager. Finally I got up enough nerve and went into the theater and asked for Mrs Moore. I almost went through the floor when her husband yelled to her that the little boy they had met in Waco was there to see her.

She greeted me and said, "I don't remember your name, but can I call you Willie?" I was so excited that I said, yes, and she took me into the theater. Mrs Moore asked me to stay and see the show, but I told her that I would have to go home and see what my mother would say. I ran home and got my mother and brother, and away we went to the show. Sure enough, as big as day, there was Blind Lemon Jefferson walking up Central Tracks, stopping wherever he could get a crowd. He started off with another of his favorites: "The blues jumped a rabbit and run him a solid mile, the rabbit sat down and cried like a natural chile." He was some showman and really went over with the crowds. We had a good time that night and Mrs Moore told my mother that I was welcome to come to the theater any time and she would look out for me.

One day, while I was walking with my brother near our home on Cochran Street, I saw a lady standing in her front yard. She called to us and said, "Would you boys like to earn some money?" My brother answered, no, but I knew the few pennies would help out at home, so I said, "Doing what?" She explained that it was helping in the house and raking the leaves and so forth. I could hear a player piano in the background. They were in vogue then, and people who had a few dollars had them; I guess you could buy it now and pay for it later. So I said that I would do the work for her on Saturdays if she would let me practice on her piano. We made a deal that she would give me lunch and a dollar and let me practice as long as I wanted to. I jumped at this chance and in a few weeks I was picking out melodies.

To those of you who may not know, a player piano is an instrument with a keyboard like a regular piano, and the motor, which is worked by pumping air with the feet, is on the inside. The upper face of the piano can be opened with two slide panels, and a piano roll is slipped into a slot on each side of the slide panels. There is a lever which you can push to start, and another to rewind the roll. There is also a button which you press to make the keys go down as if someone was playing. So excited was I to get into Mrs Lizzie Bailey's parlor, I could hardly finish the work.

Up until this time, remembering what the music teacher had said had kept me from trying to get started in music, but the moment I sat down at that player piano I felt at ease. It was a nice feeling – like a cowboy sitting in the saddle. I decided then that I would learn something about the piano – not with a teacher, but by memory. I could see the keys going down, so I remembered in sequence where each note would come. After several weeks I could play *My Isle of Golden Dreams*, note for note. As long as I live, I shall never forget the words of Mother Bailey when she heard me play her favorite song, *My Isle of Golden Dreams*. "Brother," she said, "you are doing just fine."

Mother Bailey's encouragement caused me to develop a strong wish to prove to myself and, most of all, to my mother that Professor Cobb was wrong about me. I also developed a strong will to learn, because Mother Bailey had given me a chance. You may not be able to understand what it was like to have a chance. For the first time in my life I was able to enjoy all the modern conveniences – a bathroom, electric lights, a phonograph and a piano. Coming from a poor family where we had to sleep, eat, play and live in one or two rooms, the home of Mother Bailey was luxurious. My brother and I made this our second home during the day, and Mother Bailey never complained about my practicing so much.

Then I went to Mrs Portia Pittman, the daughter of Booker T. Washington, and she started teaching me. She said to me when she first heard me touch the piano – you know, she wanted to see how much I knew and how I could play little things – she said, "Sammy, you have an exceptional feeling for the instrument." That was exactly what she said to me, and I was proud of the compliment. That was kind of unusual, because at that time music teachers were very strict – you know, "Why didn't you see that accidental? That's a B flat," and so forth. She never said that to me, and I always paid attention to her. I finally got the keyboard in my mind and I was going like a house on fire. I started asking what the names of the chords were, how to form a major chord, a minor chord, a seventh chord, an augmented chord, and on down the line.

After a while I was still taking lessons from Mrs Pittman, but I think she could smell a rat. Whenever I took a lesson she would always play the new lesson for me. I never practiced my lesson, but when I would come the next week I would always remember what she had played and play the lesson. Finally one day Mrs Pittman said, "Sammy, you have a natural talent. I don't know if you'll ever become a great technical reading musician, but you can share your natural ability and talent with other musicians who are trained." That was my last formal lesson.

I tried out my piano ideas at the home of any friend who had a piano, like Dave Allen, Martha Turner, and L. A. and C. E. Smith. Since I could now play the piano, I became very popular. This got me and my brother many invitations to parties. Originally I would just fool around and improvise. I like to think that I taught myself before others.

The junior members of the church choir would gather at Bethel AME Church on Leonard Street for rehearsal on Friday afternoons. We knew that the pianist, Fannie Gibbs, would not get there from school, where she taught, until 20 minutes after the children arrived, so we would ask Louie Fields, the son of the sexton, to get the keys to the piano. While the other children watched, we would play some real low-down blues in church.

2

Traveling the TOBA

It was in the fall of 1921 that mother wanted to know what all the talk was about that I could play the piano. I told her I could play a little, so on Christmas I got a piano for a present, which pleased me very much. By now I really was leading a full life. I used to go over to the Riverside Park in Dallas. This is where I first heard the *Michigan Water Blues* played by a localite by the name of Harry Nelson. He also taught me some other blues. I still did odd jobs for Mother Bailey, went to Ella B. Moore's theater to see the shows, and went to dances, and still found time to go to school and do my homework. Mrs Moore liked me and always let me in the theater for nothing. She asked me one day how I would like to go on the stage. I told her I could not sing or dance. She said, "You will learn. I hear you always fooling around with my piano." To me this was good news. Working as a dancer, I would have a chance to meet all the stars that came to the theater and try to learn something from each one of them. I met Sippie Wallace, Hersal Thomas, Ida Cox, Jesse Crump, Texas Alexander, Victoria Spivey, Butterbeans and Susie, and all the members of the shows that traveled over the TOBA. The TOBA circuit was similar to the Orpheum circuit for the various white shows that traveled; they had this TOBA (Theater Owners' Booking Association – though we knew it as Tough On Black Asses) for colored.

The TOBA shows that toured in the South always stopped over in Dallas. It was hard for the musicians to find accommodation, and most of them had to stay in rooming houses or private homes. I had talked my mother into putting up these touring musicians in our home so that I could maybe learn something from them. One night at Mrs

Moore's theater I met Willie Lewis, the piano player with the Blue Devils orchestra. I asked my mother if he could spend the night with us so that he could show me something about the blues. I got him out of bed around seven in the morning. All he did was laugh and say, "Sammy, I like your spirit."

In 1923 the charleston dance came out. I became an exceptional charleston dancer. Now doing these dances did one thing for me. It taught me to have confidence before an audience. I'm saying that dancing in front of people gave me confidence. I hear people call it stage fright – you know, being before an audience, being afraid, being nervous, forgetting the words if you sing, forgetting part of the routine if you're a dancer, forgetting the notes if you're a musician. Well, that dancing did quite a bit for me. It furthered my musical career.

It was in the summer of 1925 that I first heard the Alphonso Trent Orchestra in front of Ella B. Moore's theater advertising for a dance. In his band he had Terrence Holder and Chester Clark (trumpets), Snub Mosley (trombone), A. G. Godley (drums), Brent Sparks (tuba), Wendell Holloway (tenor), Gene Crook (guitar), and John Fielding (singer). Trent himself played piano. This was the first organized band that I heard, and I gave it an 'A' rating. The guys were playing together and playing different things and going from one key to another and really swinging. Trent started with about five musicians and went on to become a 12- or 14-piece band with Stuff Smith conducting. However, as great as they were, and as great as they played together, they never went to New York City. Actually, Snub Mosley said they did go to New York and were playing theaters or something, and they were asked by Meyer Davis to go into the Arcadia, which was competition to the Roseland, and he said Trent didn't want to do it because he was afraid of losing his men. He thought if they were in New York too long the good guys would quit, which Snub said they wouldn't do because they all loved Trent and they would have stayed with him. But he was kind of nervous about that, so instead they moved on. They bypassed New York City for Buffalo. That's amazing. I think if they had stayed in New York history would have been rewritten as far as fame is concerned. Everybody who really heard that band talks about how great they were, even though the records could never do them justice because of the inferior quality of recordings in those days.

It was from Trent's band that I got the idea of organizing Salesman Sam and his Syncopated Six. By now Mother had taken a larger house with a parlor and everything, so I asked her one day to make sandwiches and lemonade for the fellows I had invited down to my house. There was Budd Johnson, Booker Pittman, Herman Batts, John R. Davis, Willie Owens and myself. I did not tell them what the party was all about until after we had finished the refreshments. When I told them my plans for the Syncopated Six they all said, no. I ran outside and got my gang of friends and chased them out of my neighborhood. I was determined this would not stop me.

Bert Goldberg, who was the manager of Alphonso Trent's orchestra, came with Trent to a dance in the black community. He saw me dancing out on the floor and everybody crowded around me. When you're a crowd-pleaser, such can happen. He said to Trent, "Why don't we take that dancer and let him dance with the band when they play the Adolphus Hotel or some big white place? White people want to see a black kid dancing." And I really could do the charleston. The charleston had become such a rage across America that if you could do it, and do it well, you were *it* in those days. They decided that I would go to Mineral Wells or Austin or Houston or wherever they'd play. I jumped at the offer, as it would give me a chance to be around the band, and I was sure I could learn something from the men. I could go in with the band and sit behind the piano until the time for me to appear and do my charleston. The band would pay me, and then I'd make a lot of tips. This is how I really broke into what I call the local big time.

One of the things that happened sitting behind that piano for three or four hours was that I had an opportunity to really listen to musical changes: hear a guy play a different kind of

solo, or hear the trumpets coming in, or the piano playing –
this is a piano solo or a clarinet solo. I had an opportunity
during this period with Trent to learn these things, which
didn't hurt. Trent was a fine musician. He liked me, and he
used to teach me things. Wherever we would go, say we
were playing the Adolphus Hotel, we might arrive at the
place an hour before, you understand, and he might be
practicing or learning a new song or arrangement. I could sit
in the rehearsals. I began to hear things like, "That's a B flat;
tune your horn," and that business. I learned things about
music and about the piano - how to play soft, tonal quality
and, you know, various rhythms and that sort of thing. That
really started me. I made little notes, and then you couldn't
stop me.

Earlier, before I really knew what I was doing, I had so
much nerve that when a guy came looking for a piano player
to play for some man, I said I played the piano. The guy took
me up to this club, and this man was sitting there with a
bottle of whiskey, and he said, "Play me some music." I
played *My Isle of Golden Dreams*. Then he said, "OK, now
play me some blues." I played *My Isle of Golden Dreams*. He
says, "OK, play me something with the charleston." I played
My Isle . . .. He told me, "Get the hell out of here," and he
gave me five dollars. That was the first.

But my first real job came in 1925. By this time there was
talk that "Sam Price is dancing with the Alphonso Trent
Band," and "Sam Price has learned, man, he's playing the
piano," and this, that and the other. I could play the
charleston by now, and you know I could play *My Isle of
Golden Dreams*. Whatever there was, I'd play these things,
most of the time with the wrong notes. So finally this man
came to me and said he wanted me to come to Athens,
Texas, to play for a dance. He'd pay me five dollars a night
for a Saturday and Sunday, plus round-trip transportation
and room and board. I made a big hit there and was home in
time for Christmas dinner – I like to eat. I thought I was a big
man then. It was just me and the piano, and it was out of
tune, but it was the first professional job I had.

In 1925 I was also very, very close to Ella B. Moore. I'd stand around the theater when Cow Cow Davenport came to town, and Jesse Crump, my favorite, and others who played for Ida Cox. Jesse "Tiny" Crump was Ida Cox's husband. You couldn't call him tiny, though. He was a big, immaculate man, dressed nice – silk shirt, tie, watch fob and tie clasp, shoes shined. He was great. When Jesse came to town I would always be hanging around the theater as they arrived, and I would stay until they left. I watched everything and tried to be just as professional in that way. Actually I was improving my piano playing. People were letting me play now and then, and at house-rent parties I was popular, very popular. One night, while I was sitting in with Mrs Moore, Ida Cox was on stage with Jesse Crump at the piano. I almost went through the floor when she announced my name and said I was a fine piano player and asked me to come on stage and play a song with her. She didn't know that Jesse Crump was my favorite blues piano player, and that I had learned all the songs that he had recorded with her. I played two songs with her, playing the parts just as Mr Crump played on the records. We made a big hit with the *Death Letter Blues* and *Hard, oh Lord*.

The spring of 1927 found me getting ready to go on the road with Mrs Moore and a little show that she had got together made up of young people, all from Dallas. I could dance and this gave me the opportunity to go. The kids were pretty good, though, doing little drama things, and we had chorus girls and so on. There was Irene Moore, Dorothy Mays, Helen Morrison, Ishmael Watkins, Paula Moore, Tiny Durham, Herman Odham, Harrison Blackburn, Lorraine Winn, Mrs Vivian Moore of Little Rock, Arkansas, as the piano player, and yours truly, dancer and actor. Show people then used to wear shoes without laces; there were no strings. You took a shoe horn and put the shoe on, but it was just like these shoes I have now – there was no tongue; they had a top, but there wasn't anything on it. So the first thing I did when Mrs Moore said, "Go on the show," was to go buy me a pair of those shoes like the road-show stars.

We played dates in Ardmore, Texas, and Okmulgee and Tulsa in Oklahoma. In Okmulgee I first met Oscar Pettiford, the bass player. He was three years of age at that time, almost a baby. They had a family band and a little amusement park. Okmulgee was also where I first met Count Basie. He was in the Gonzelle White show with two trumpet players – I think they were Guy Kelly from New Orleans and a guy named Zeddie. This was before Basie went to Kansas City. I remember it was the first time that I ever saw a hundred-dollar bill. Gonzelle White had it. In Tulsa we first met Jimmy Rushing, who was singing with the Blue Devils band. Buster Smith was also with them, and Hot Lips Page joined them in Tulsa. I had seen Hot Lips Page before when I went with several fellows to Corsicana to see a football game; Lips was in the grandstand blowing some fine trumpet, and it was not long after that that he joined the Blue Devils. Harry Smith was with the show too.

Then I just became excited. I was playing more and more, although not for money. I just used to play. Especially if they came to me and said, "It's bad, and we want you to play tonight, will you help us out?" As they'd have seven or eight musicians, they didn't get much money anyway. I'd give my share to the others. I could go some place and dance and get extra money, or I could gamble – I knew all those things. So I would go and play with the musicians. Budd Johnson and Buster Smith, Dan Minor, a trombone player, John R. Davis and Willie Owens were all local musicians, but they were well known. You had another segment in Dallas, like the bandleaders Troy Floyd and Benny Long, people like that who were local favorites. Benno Kennedy was a fantastic trumpet player, and a really nice person. He played with Trent.

I think that playing music can be contagious, and then, if you have any insight at all, you're fascinated. That damn guy who said I didn't know anything about music was crazy, because he didn't realize that I had this innate feeling for music. The moment Mrs Bailey asked me to do that work, I think that's when I came alive. I just decided to try. What did he mean telling me that I didn't have feeling? I think that anybody can learn something. For example, they say the white musicians can't play, but I don't want anybody telling me Gene Krupa wasn't a good musician. I don't want them telling me that Benny Goodman, no matter if he was classically trained, wasn't a good musician. I think because we think in the tradition of heritage, of black heritage, that may be the thing that people have not been able to unscramble. In black jazz, writers need to determine what we're talking about. See, we're talking about black jazz here; when we speak of jazz, then we speak of a thing that's a black creation, but that doesn't mean that it has to necessarily remain that. Then we believe that there should be those original roots.

Lee Collins also came to Dallas that year with a band from New Orleans. A lot of New Orleans musicians used to come up there, but a whole New Orleans band would only come up and stay for a special event or a dance somewhere like the North Dallas Club, or Riverside Park, or the big dance hall over the river. I saw John Robichaux, Papa Celestin – people like that. So when Lee Collins came to Dallas he had Percy Darensbourg on guitar. Percy later became a big nightclub guy – not an entertainer, but selling whiskey and stuff. Then there was Freddy Bobo on trombone, a little boy named LeRoy Williams on drums, and a man by the name of Octave Crosby on piano. Lee played trumpet. After a few days he got homesick for New Orleans and some of that gumbo. When they got like that those fellows couldn't contain themselves – they just went like insane longing for home.

So Professor Sherman Cook, who was the dancer, manager, and MC, came to my house and asked me if I would play some dates with the band. This was the hardest job I ever played. We had to travel by car with all the instruments to Wichita Falls, Texas, to play for three nights. I explained to the band before I left Dallas that I could not read music. I said, "Now look, I'm no piano player when it comes down to this business. But if you start a song off, after you play the first few notes, then I can come in. But don't depend on me to come in leading it." This was OK with them.

The minute we got on the job all this changed. They'd

bring the music: "Now in the fourteenth bar you will do this and do that." And when I could not answer, they would talk in a broken French to each other. They did that to me for two or three days. I told them, "Don't you mess with me," but they kept it up. To tell you the truth, I wanted to hurt one of them. When we started to play, the piano was so out of tune we had to play cross. What I mean is, if we played a song in B flat, I would have to play in B natural in order to be in tune with the band. I was glad to get back to Dallas. After the show we all got into this big black Cadillac, and they started on me again, talking that patois. I got tired of their shit and I said, "I told you not to mess with me." I pulled out my gun and they all tried to get out of the car while it was moving. I ran them all down the highway and wouldn't let them come back to the car. The guys that were the managers were coming in a car behind us and they saw all these Frenchmen running. It was funny. So finally Cal Liston said, "Put that gun away," and I got in the car with the managers and went back to Dallas. It certainly taught them a lesson. The guy driving the car, Trembling Slim, tried to tell them that I was one of the Price boys, and if I did not win them, they would have to meet my brother.

There had not been much recording at that time. During those days you had Bessie Smith, Ida Cox and Ma Rainey, who were popular girl singers, and Bert Williams. Incidentally, let me tell you a story. By now, Mamie Smith had made her famous *Crazy Blues* (composed by Perry "Mule" Bradford, who later became one of my best friends). The lady that lived next door to us, Mrs Agnes, wanted to buy the record, as she had a phonograph. So it was decided that I would go to the music shop for it. Instead of my going to the black store to buy it and asking for a special record, I went to the white store and asked for the *Crazy Blues*. I had run all the way to the shop, arriving there out of breath. This guy gave me the record in a package and said, "Now if you break this, I'm not going to exchange it." So I walked very carefully home, holding it like a father would hold a new-born baby. When I reached home, the neighbors were all there to hear the record. Mrs Agnes put the record on the machine, put in a new needle, started the machine, and instead of the voice of Mamie Smith, out came Bert Williams singing the *Crazy Blues*. Everybody in the house fell about laughing. I am sure I told that man, Mamie Smith; I don't think he had ever heard of her.

The Ashford Record Shop was on the Central Tracks in the center of the black neighborhood. Actually, I don't think Mr Ashford could make it just selling records, so he had a shoeshine parlor – sold shoelaces and things. He had about seven guys shining shoes. I used to work there because the people wanted the Charleston King to shine their shoes. So you see, all through life I've always tried to figure how to stay one step ahead of the poverty line. Those kind of record stores were around a lot down South. Shoeshining was a real, real lucrative business for Blacks, because it was one thing that you could make some money on with very little investment.

Mr Ashford used to get talent. He had a woman named Hattie Burleson, a singer – and Victoria Spivey, she was another local talent. Now, Blind Lemon Jefferson had been the first blues singer that I had paid attention to, so I went to Mr Ashford one day and said, "You know, Mr Ashford, I think Blind Lemon Jefferson would sound good on records." And he said, "Mmmmh." He never indicated to me that he would negotiate. He got together with the record company, and that's how Blind Lemon Jefferson made his first record. And I didn't get anything for it. I can think that I had something to do with it, because the next year they recorded Coley Jones, who played the mandolin, and Texas Alexander, a blues singer who I trained, since he never could carry a tune. Now there's a guy who didn't know anything about music. Texas Alexander had no conception; he didn't know when to start and when to stop, or anything. Therefore I was able to help him quite a bit. I would call him a real primitive blues singer, while Blind Lemon Jefferson was what we now call a country blues artist.

It was in the fall of 1927 that Travis Tucker and Happy

Donovan's road show came to town on the TOBA. When the show was ready to move on to the next town, Houston, they were short of three people. I had been hanging around Ella B. Moore's theater with my friend Leonard Reed, a dancer, who was in town with his wife Ola. (Leonard used to be very, very close with Joe Louis, the boxer, and was later the manager of the Apollo Theater in Harlem.) The three of us decided to join the show, which was called *Let's Go Get Happy*, to help out. They had contracts, and this contract called for 20 people; the man would be at the station to count heads, and, if you didn't have 20 people, he would not pay you. He'd let you sing and dance all week long, then he would tell you that your contract called for 20 people, and he would legally fire you. We left Dallas with the show.

Leonard, Ola, Happy, Travis, myself, and a whole slew of TOBA favorites went from Dallas to Houston. Now, I'd been playing shows – you know, amateur – for Mrs Moore, but this was my first professional show. We rehearsed all day. Happy Donovan's wife, Clara, liked me and said that she would help me with the music, and I said, "Well, I can't play the music fast enough. There's jazz and stuff." So she said, "What you do, I'll hum. When a number comes up and they say, 'and now so-and-so singing the blues,' I'll start humming backstage, and when you hear me you can start the music from that." That's how I played my first week as a professional person on the TOBA, with her help. When it came to the tempos, she said, "I'll stomp." She'd start, and I could hear the tempo; I'd pick it up from her and her humming, and start the song. That was the thing about the TOBA. If you had a professional show and an amateur came along, they'd just stick him in there like he was a pro, and in no time flat he'd learn.

While we were in Houston, Hersal Thomas the blues player, Sippie Wallace's brother, always had two or three women following him around. We were friends, so after the show one night we went to this after-hours club, and when we got there he tried to show me up by telling everybody how great a piano player he was and that I couldn't play as well as him. So I said, "Man, you don't want to mess with me." I said, "Hersal, you know I'm too good for you. I'm from the 'Big D'." So finally he kept fooling around and fooling around, so I said, "OK, I'll play." When I sat down I played his most popular recording, *Suitcase Blues*, note for note, having learned it from his record. When I finished the song all of his friends came over to the piano and started pulling for me. The girls treated me like I was a baby, trying to wipe my face and hugging me and asking, "Are you going to come home with me?" and all that. What I did was to confuse Hersal; I knew he was the best piano player, but I shocked him by playing his own song as well as he could play it. He played something else. Then I moved in for the kill. I played everything I knew. Then I went into my *Dallas Stomp*, the blues with rhythm. I could really stomp, because this girl Clara had really taught me. A week with her and I realized that that's what rhythm was, that the rhythm was part of the music.

When I got through with that number, that was the end of Mr Hersal's popularity, and when the show left Houston I was very popular with the blues lovers. Hersal followed me from Houston to Galveston. Every time he challenged me I would do the same thing. He didn't have the sense enough to sit down and be the first to play the thing that he wrote. He'd follow me to a town and when I'd sit down I'd say, "Hersal, I told you . . .," and I'd play the *Suitcase Blues*. They just couldn't believe it. I think I broke his heart, though maybe I just hurt his feelings. By then, after the second week, I was a veteran. I could play the blues much better because I knew Jesse Crump's songs. I learned how to develop a system of chords. You know those guitar parts and banjo parts where they have the names of the chords, well I devised a way that I could take a piece of newspaper and write down the chords on it. Then I learned the structure of the chords – what the tonic note was and so forth.

Well, I had learned all that from Mrs Pittman, but I learned much more playing blues and boogie-woogie movement – though we didn't call it that. It was called walking bass. The first time I heard it called boogie-woogie was when Pine Top Smith recorded for Mayo Williams in 1928 out of Chicago. It was that same bass movement Blind Lemon Jefferson played on his guitar, but *he* called it booga-rooga. I don't know how you can explain these terms, how descriptions fall into a certain category and become a certain thing, but it was booga-rooga for Blind Lemon Jefferson. He played those movements, those boogie-woogie movements, and those eighth-notes.

We left Galveston, and Hersal with a broken heart, and went to Shreveport. Shreveport is where I first met Lannie Scott and George Lewis the clarinetist. Professor Campbell had the band, in the Star Theater. From Shreveport we went to Mobile, Alabama. All the time, each week, we were meeting different people: different shows of 10, 20, or 30 people. When we got to Louisville, that's where I first met Art Tatum. Later Art and I became close friends, really good pals, but after 1928 I didn't see him until I saw him in Chicago with Adelaide Hall in the early 1930s. I think Joe Turner was with Adelaide at that time. At one time she had Art and Joe at the same time. When I first heard Art he was already playing that same style, but I didn't think he could play as well as Lannie Scott. I learned my lesson. When I was in Chicago later I went to this after-hours spot, and Lovey Taylor said to Earl Hines, "Earl, there's a kid in town playing the piano. Like to hear him?"

Earl said, "No, I don't want to hear nobody." So Art Tatum started playing *Tiger Rag*. It was just amazing. You just couldn't believe that one man could play that fast, or do as much, or have as much speed; he seemed ambidextrous, musically developed beyond description. Art Tatum was my inspiration. I could never play like Art, and I don't even sound like him, but the ideas that he had was what I like to hear. He was just so amazing. From then on Art and I became very, very close. I have a picture that I cherish of Art Tatum and myself and Teddy Wilson. Now, the picture is all right, but do you know who's sitting at the piano? I'm sitting at the piano, and Teddy and Art are looking down at me playing.

From Mobile we went to Atlanta. In Atlanta Graham Jackson was playing the organ in the 81 Theater. Eddie Heywood, Sr, was in town (Eddie Heywood, Jr, was not around at that time). From there we went to Memphis, where I think we saw Lovie Austin. Then I met W. C. Handy in Memphis.

When you traveled on the TOBA you had problems. For example, in Atlanta they had two shows a night, and then on Friday they'd have a midnight show. Now you weren't supposed to be on the street after midnight in Atlanta at that time if you were black. If you forgot to get your letter or your pass from the boss man who owned the 81 Theater stating that you were going home from work, they put you in jail and held you overnight. Sometimes they'd put a guy in jail and he'd be wanted for some crime someplace else, so you had to be very careful. I've known many nights that guys would stay in the theater all night. They'd stay in the dressing room, sleeping on the floor.

In Pensacola, Florida, if you went on the stage and didn't have pantyhose - opera lengths, they called them – that's stockings covering the legs, they'd put you in jail for that. But if you went to jail in Pensacola they'd let you out to do the show. Then you'd have to go back to jail. Like if a guy gets three days in jail for doing something, they'd let him come out and do the show, and then he'd spend the rest of the night in jail.

On the TOBA there was very little money, but people didn't mind. They would get a room and board, that is one meal a day – dinner served between five and seven; you'd eat half of it and put the other half in a doggy bag. If you were lucky, you'd get a few dollars when the shows played some cities. It was a very interesting training ground. It was like a *Who's Who in America* – or Black America – because if they were anybody in black entertainment, they traveled the TOBA. From George Williams and Bessie Brown to Bert Williams, Ma Rainey, and Trixie Smith, they were all there. Ella Fitzgerald wasn't around in those days – this TOBA was before her time. But this was the big route of the blues: Bessie Smith, Eddie Heywood, Sr, Clara Smith, Pine Top

Smith, Sara Martin and Victoria Spivey were some of the top stars of the day, along with Ma Rainey and Trixie Smith. Space will not allow me to name all the little singers that I had a chance to hear from October 1927 to Christmas 1928.

Coot Grant and Sox Wilson had a show on the TOBA circuit that toured under their name. It had chorus girls and a couple of dancers, maybe a singer, and what we called a straight man. Every show had a straight man, who actually could be called the announcer. He did the talking, the straight talk: "Good evening, ladies and gentlemen. And now we present the dancing girls." And they'd come out and dance. And after that they'd have a comedian do a skit, all that kind of stuff. Coot Grant and Sox Wilson would do a dialogue scene. There'd be a situation like where there was a man gets up to go to work and his wife fixes lunch for him, and when he goes out the door he forgets the lunch. Well, he's gone long enough for her Sweet Poppa Charlie to come in, then when they hear somebody knock on the door, then the guy would get out of the bed and go out, but say something like, "Wait a minute, I forgot my scarf." You know, funny skits like that. That was the kind of humor that was popular in those days. Coot Grant and Sox Wilson was big in the early 1930s. They sang on some of Mezz Mezzrow's records, too.

Most of towns that the TOBA covered were in the Southwest. There was a circuit, and you'd start occasionally in Chicago, but mostly in St Louis. Then you'd go to Kansas City, from Kansas City to Tulsa, from Tulsa to Oklahoma City, from Oklahoma City to Dallas, from Dallas to Houston, from Houston to Galveston, from Galveston to Shreveport, from Shreveport to Mobile, then Pensacola, Atlanta, Jacksonville, Cincinnati, Washington, Chattanooga, Nashville, Birmingham, Durham, Louisville, Danville, Lynchburg, Baltimore, Norfolk, Newport News and Memphis. A lot of the time shows would break up in Washington. You had maybe 15 weeks. It was very, very interesting, and the thing that it taught you – and I still have the same fidelity today – is to have a lot of respect for each other, for your fellow performer.

For example, if a guy was sick and he lived in Houston, and we were in Tulsa, we'd take care of him in Tulsa, Oklahoma City and Dallas, and on the fourth week we'd deliver him to his people in Houston. If you wanted to send money, you'd say, "Now, when you get down in Shreveport, give this to my aunt and stay with her that week." Maybe coming from the other way, Louisville, you'd come back down to Winston-Salem and all, until you got to Shreveport and you'd give the money to the aunt of the friend, and so forth. I also learned how to send a message to a loved one in a distant city and rest assured that the person would receive it. The TOBA taught you fidelity, friendship, respect and recognition, plus training; these things, and many more, are what you learned, and I'm sure you will agree with me that sometimes they are more important than money. Where else could you practice a profession before audiences who have paid to see and hear you perform, until you become perfect? Although I didn't receive money, I learned much while traveling with the TOBA and was able to perfect my talent before appreciative crowds; to me, that was worth more than any monetary compensation. There should be another TOBA today – it would help the youngsters. Black Americans need these training grounds.

You know, during those years, singers were the principals. You don't think Coleman Hawkins could have taken his tenor saxophone and gone out on stage and stood in front of Butterbeans and Susie and been the star? He was just another musician in the background. *Maybe* they'd let him play a number. Maybe. Or he'd have an opportunity to play when the chorus girls were featured. Then you could really do your thing and play as hard as you wanted to, which would be an inspiration to the chorus girls. Other than that, very seldom would you have a band that was the attraction and actually featured. I can't remember when they ever did that on the TOBA. It's quite possible, but I'm telling you from my knowledge what they would do. A guy would come on the show. He could play when the chorus girls were dancing, you know, do his thing. When George Williams and Bessie Brown came out to sing one of those songs, or Ida

Cox had a solo, or Bessie Smith was singing the *Back Water Blues*, there was no place for an instrumental soloist, because James P. Johnson had set the precedent, on records. Very rarely did people stray from that original format.

You know, you had bands like McKinney's Cotton Pickers. Speaking of McKinney's Cotton Pickers, Fletcher Henderson played dances, though not in the South, because there were not so many halls for them to play. Local bands – territory bands they called them – like the Blue Devils, Alphonso Trent, Troy Floyd, Benny Long, Bennie Moten, and Andy Kirk with the Twelve Clouds of Joy – these were the bands that really played. You rarely saw Duke Ellington in Dallas during that period. He played New York, say the Cotton Club, or Chicago, then went to California to Sebastian's or something like that.

Then in 1927, when the Regal Theater in Chicago opened, they'd have a show. They always had to have that original TOBA format of a comedian – Pigmeat Markham or Bert Williams (though Bert didn't play too many black theaters). Then they also had Trixie Smith, Ida Cox, Mamie Smith, Eldora Williams, and many other blues singers, and each of these blues singers would have a person with them who played exclusively for them. Like Ida Cox would have Jesse Crump and Ma Rainey had Thomas A. Dorsey. George Williams and Bessie Brown, and Butterbeans and Susie, they used the show piano player. You very rarely had, like, stars. Now Pine Top Smith was one who played for the whole show. It's too bad he got killed so early because he was really something to behold. He was playing that very simple boogie-woogie.

3

Going to Kansas City

I've yet to tell you how I got my first wife, which was on that
TOBA tour. We left Memphis and went to Danville, Virginia,
with the show, and a man by the name of Boise DeLegge
came into town at the same time we were there. People used
to try to steal – not steal, but entice – people from one show
to another. The show that we were on needed four more
people. In the other show there was a guy named Joseph
Hubert, the guy who wrote *I'm falling for you*, and his wife
and two dancers. We met at this restaurant and we were
talking about how people didn't get any money – the
managers just didn't pay you because they didn't have it.
And we asked Joe Hubert to leave Boise DeLegge and come
with Happy Donovan and Travis Tucker. He said, all right,
he'd do it.

Well, somehow Boise DeLegge found out that Joe was
going to leave the show, and Joe was trying to hide around.
Boise was from New Orleans and with a hot temper, and he
belted Joe one right in the eye. Well, Joe was ready to stay
with the show, but naturally, with people all agitating about
it, he said, "Well, you haven't paid me for the last eight
weeks." That was the only way he could get away from the
show, because the guy knew he hadn't paid him.

Boise DeLegge also had a Japanese girl in the show named
Louise Attrisbird. I took her for my old lady, and Boise didn't
dare get out of line because he had heard about me. On the
TOBA shows, if there were five chorus girls that were single
and there were five men that were single, before the evening
was over you would have five marriages – not shotgun, but
performed by the manager. That was because he would save
the cost of five rooms. An economic solution. So if you were

married or lived in common law, just sleeping with a person in a room, then that was just one room. So there we were in this hotel in Danville, when the place was raided: "Everybody out in the hallway." Well, five doors opened, and here are ten people. The man said, "Now, if this is your wife, I want to see the marriage license. And if it's not your wife, you're going to jail." Well, when I got down to the jail the manager of the show put up a bond. We had to leave Virginia, because I was not 21, and go to North Carolina, get married, and then bring that license back to Virginia and present it to the judge to get the money back on the bond.

Well, what I should have done, when they let me out of jail, I should have kept running as fast as I could. But I was going to be a man, and I took the thing seriously. I was going to get married and have a home and save money, though it was hard to do any of these things with the man not paying you. You were lucky if you got a room and some food. So we got married.

My wife ran away after three weeks. We were playing the 81 Theater in Atlanta, Georgia. Some guy with a nice suit and a few bucks came in on the show that was behind us. So she ran away to a pinstripe, stayed away three weeks. When I caught up with her and the guy, I threatened him: "What do you mean by this? That's my wife!"

He tried to apologize: "I didn't mean no harm." You know the business – all that stuff. I took her back, and so we left Atlanta and went on to some other cities, and we ended up in Pittsburgh. And in Pittsburgh the show that I was on broke up and I couldn't feed her.

But I did feed her, because Leonard Reed and myself became pool sharks. Leonard was an excellent pool player. So we would go to a local pool room – two strangers – and I would beat him, because I can shoot pretty good, and I would be winning all of the money. Now the local guys would see how easy he was to beat, and they asked me to let them play. And when they played he would beat them out of their money. The old hustler's trick.

So what happened was, there was a woman in town who

had a show, and she liked me. I was always half slick with women, that was my thing. I could out-talk anyone and it would sound convincing. The lady was very, very nice to me. And Louise was eating good. And one day Louise asked me, "Where are you getting this money?" I told her I was getting the money from Lena Horne's father, Teddy Horne, who lived in Pittsburgh.

So one night after work I made a mistake. Every night I used to leave home at around six in time for dinner at this woman's house, and then I'd get some money and come back and feed my friends. So when I left my room, my wife followed me. And when I rang this lady's doorbell, there she was. And she was going to kill herself, then me, and then the other woman and everyone else she saw. And the woman had a cat that didn't like me, so I couldn't go indoors because that cat would try to jump on me, and my wife was outside going to kill me. So the following day we were hungry again. I'd just frozen on that doorstep and said to my wife, "C'mon, let's settle this out of court!"

Well, a show came through and, as I said, they always need people. So we got on the show and went from Pittsburgh to Washington. I tried one time to become a comedian in Washington: they said, "Yeah, we need a comedian." So I got on the show and the man said, "Well, you're a comedian," and he gave me my lines. I looked real stupid. I walked out on the stage and I was supposed to say, "Are you there?" And the woman was supposed to answer to that, "Yes, you're there. You'd better stay there. You're a big black bear." Just like that. You know, I couldn't remember those words. I got fired from that. Anyway, we got stranded again in Washington, so we got on another show back to Texas, where my home was (Louise was from Chicago), and at Christmas 1928 we ended up back in Dallas. We got home just in time for Christmas dinner, and we ate like horses. I was glad to get a good dinner – turkey and all that business – and I was so glad to be home.

The only thing wrong with Louise was that she thought she was Joe Louis, the fighter. And she'd take me on, too,

but she didn't have the strength to win. I could just hold her.
But she broke up all of my mother's dishes and fine little
things, and this just destroyed my mother's living room. We
fought all over the place, all through the back and everything. So finally I said, "You know not to be here when my
mother comes." (Because my mother liked to fight, too, and
she would take care of my brother and all.) And when my
mother came home, Louise left, and that was when we split,
in 1929. I saw her once more, in Chicago in 1932. And then I
got a divorce from her.

It was while I was in Dallas that I made my first
recordings. That was October 1929, for J. Mayo Williams. I
had Bert Johnson on trombone, Percy Darensbourg on guitar
and banjo and a trumpeter that was called Kid Lips, and we
called the band Sam Price and his Four Quarters. We did *Blue
Rhythm Stomp*, and *Nasty but Nice* with Effie Scott making
comments.

I decided after a while that the traveling fever was in my
blood. It's pretty rugged to live in the South in some small
town after you've experienced St Louis and Washington and
Louisville and all those fast towns, and seen Ida Cox and
Trixie Smith and Mamie Smith, and I got the feeling of being
somebody more important than just going over to some local
dance hall and hear some guy play, hear somebody sing that
is really amateur. I just felt that I was above that.

Another show came to Dallas, and I went to Tulsa, then
from Tulsa to Oklahoma City. My brother was in jail in the
locality, in Ada. He was a pseudo desperado, always doing
the wrong thing. So I went back to my thing of getting a writ.
I got a writ of habeas corpus and got him out of jail, and we
went to Oklahoma City. We had to have food and we had to
have a room. So I went to this friend of mine named Jales
Scales that owned a restaurant and asked Mr Scales how
he'd like to have his restaurant advertised on the radio. He
looked at me like I was crazy. "What station?"

"KFJF." That was a good station. He looked at me and
said, "How you goin' to do this?"

"Don't worry. Leave it to me."

I went to the radio station, asked the man how he'd like to have some music on his station at 12 o'clock during the day, and *he* looked at me like I was crazy. But he took me on, and I announced the restaurant over the radio. I was with Lem Johnson and Leonard Chadwick. We did *Funky Butt* and the switchboard lit up – the guy was taking calls left and right. He was so excited. And he yelled to me, "What's the name of the band?" We didn't have a name, so I just said, "Lemuel C, Samuel B and Leonard C." Just made up the initials and gave him a name. We were very popular and ended up staying there for three weeks.

Well, I had that drifting blood, and finally I told the man I had to go to Kansas City because I had a big record transaction coming up, and I sent my brother back to Dallas. That was bullshit. I hardly knew anybody in Kansas City – only Buddy Tate, who was there by that time, and another kid I knew from Waco called Willie "Mack" Washington, who used to be the drummer with Bennie Moten. I'd met Lester Young down in Dallas – I'd met a lot of musicians coming through Dallas – and Eddie Durham. That was the same year I met Alphonso Trent, in 1925. Eddie was just playing trombone at that time, not guitar. He had a thing called the Durham Brothers Band, and they were all brothers – except one, I think, who was a cousin. These musicians weren't on the circuit; they used to come to the most lucrative towns where they could put on a dance. And Dallas was a sizable town with a black population.

Anyway, I wanted to go to Kansas City, but this woman who liked my music came up to me and pulled out a .45 and told me that if I tried to leave town she'd kill me. Well, thank God for kidneys! When she went to the bathroom and I just took off.

This was Kansas City when Count Basie was there, and it meant nothing to see him. But it was Kansas City, which to me at that point was the highlight – not the climax, but the highlight. It was such an exciting city; it had become the jazz capital overnight. You'd have Julia Lee, George Lee, Andy Kirk, Mary Lou Williams, Hot Lips Page, Dan Minor, Budd

Johnson, Keg Johnson, Booker Pittman, Buster Smith, Walter Page, Vic Dickenson, Jack Washington, Jimmy Rushing, Big Joe Turner, Eddie Durham, and Pete Johnson. All of the musicians that you had known over the years and you had picked as possibly going to the top of the heap were in Kansas City. And then you had like Louis coming to town, and Don Redman, McKinney's Cotton Pickers – all of the leading attractions.

This was all fascinating to me. I couldn't really get it in my mind that here I was, Sammy Price, who the music teacher said would never play, I had no ideas. I was amazed that I found myself in the "City of Swing" with Lester Young, an amazing stylist who could not be copied. He was one of the most outstanding musicians that I've ever met; I don't ever remember having met a person that was as unique. He was sort of cute, but he was a man too – sweet, nice, polite, kind, but mean as hell. But all the good parts always came out of him at all times. Lester Young acted the part.

Stuff Smith was there at one time, but not as much. Abe Bolar the bass player was there. Jimmy Mundy was there, and Jesse Stone. We had a famous pianist named Emil Williams, and it's amazing that Benno Kennedy didn't ever come to Kansas City during the two or three years I was there. Thamon Hayes, Pha Terrell, and Tickle Toe, who was a dancer, were all around. Strange as it seems to many people, wherever there was a style of music played or a song created, they created a dance to go along with it. For example, you take the charleston. James P. Johnson wrote that song *The Charleston*. He should have become really rich, like Elvis Presley or the Rolling Stones – the charleston was well received all over the world. Now why didn't James P. have 35 million dollars? I can think of a series of songs that had a dance to go along with them; I think that the dancing and the music are so interrelated that when you think of one you have to think of the other.

In Kansas City I wasn't ever slick, because I never tried to fleece anybody or tried to sell the Brooklyn Bridge. My thing was with the ladies – I could make it with the ladies. Really, when I think of it, I don't think they made too much of a contribution. It was just that confidence which they gave me that made me, because as long as I can remember, I've always worked. So I wasn't a pimp. I wasn't living in somebody's house or having some woman keep me and come and bring my rent. I always worked. But I think that in my mind I wanted to think that I was slick. Eddie Barefield always said that every town I went in over the years, I was always there with a woman. He said, "You've *always* had a woman with you." I said, well, there was a reason for that; you know, she's probably buying the tickets. So what Eddie Barefield said, well, that's possibly true.

I was involved with a well-known shoplifter. She was a nice person, really and truly a nice person. Her name was Valetta, and she liked me. I was a piano player and I talked big, told her I was friendly with President Roosevelt and people like that. She was from Topeka, and her father was a policeman. She was very, very friendly.

You see, I was on the weak side, just trying to live. I was a compulsive gambler, and still am – right up to last night. I can't help it. I like to take every chance. I even did that in France: I won a lot of money when I was there in 1948 when Mezz's band played in Nice – that big festival when Louis was there, and Humphrey Lyttelton, Barney Bigard, Earl Hines and Baby Dodds. I think I won $10,000 at the casino. And the next day every casino in Europe was sending me some kind of invitation to go there and gamble. I think they must have some kind of mutual society – a gamblers' mutual society – to spread the word, because I was invited to gambling places all over. So in Kansas I was gambling, and Valetta was my lady. She was loaning me a little money to play, and nine times out of ten, I'd win.

I was always friendly with the operators in Kansas City, the people who owned the clubs. I was good friends with Ellis Burton, who was the owner of the Yellow Front Cafe, and Piney Brown, the manager of the Sunset Club, and Felix Payne, another patron of jazz musicians. They used to call people there gangsters and all that, but I never saw any wrongdoing. I don't know what a gangster is. I'll say this, that many of those persons that were accused of being gangsters were the ones that had nightclubs and places where musicians played, so if they were gangsters, they gave a lot of people work. If it wasn't for those fellows who had those clubs you wouldn't have any jazz at all. Prohibition had something to do with the gangster element, being involved with selling liquor, because it was illegal. Everybody drank, so they must have been getting the whiskey someplace.

Anyway, I worked. I got a job as leader of the house band at the Yellow Front – just me and Merle Johnson, a drummer. That's where I got Bunk up to play, but it was a mistake. Ellis Burton asked me who we could get from New Orleans just to have around. Ellis's place was a gambling house, held maybe 50, 60 people, and the music wasn't important; having the music was just a come-on for people. Men would bring their wives there, they'd eat in the restaurant, and then the men would go in the back to the gambling tables to play blackjack and dice. The dice game would be the biggest, and it would go on all night and all day. The place never closed. It was illegal, but Kansas City, Missouri, was wide open; things happened 24 hours a day.

So I'd do the best I could to keep the wives happy. Well, people knew Sammy Price from Texas – slick dude, smart and all that – he was popular. But the same way as when you go in a record store where you can get your shoes shined, and you hear a record and you buy it, we thought Bunk would be an attraction – that's why we got someone from New Orleans. We got Bunk Johnson, and by the time that he got there he was so darn high that he didn't know where he was. I don't think Bunk even remembered coming to Kansas City. He stayed around there two or three days and we couldn't do anything with him at all, so we sent him back to New Orleans. He tried to play, but he couldn't. He lost his coat coming up, and lost his hat going back – and his teeth. Bunk was a character, a legend. They were saying he was the guy that taught Louis, and that even then before Bill Russell and those recordings.

The other joints in Kansas City were Piney Brown's club, the Subway (at 18th Street and Vine), the Panama Club, and the Reno (which was downtown). There were other black clubs for black audiences, but there were very rarely mixed audiences. The Reno was a white club with a black band. At the Subway one night there was a jam session. I went home at nine o'clock to change, came back at one o'clock, and they were still playing the same song. The thing that I could never understand is how in the hell on weekends everybody'd go out and go into a club. By word of mouth you'd have hundreds of people gathering, and the place would be crowded. The local papers printed once a week for Blacks, so by the time the article came out on Friday or Saturday the affair would be over. But it was amazing how, by word of mouth, these performers could become so famous and so popular. People would know they were coming to town and they would crowd out the dance halls.

I stayed my time out in Kansas City, from 1929 to 1932. I felt like a disciple, that I was supposed to stay in a certain place until my time was out and then move on. I left because there was just too much competition. Basie and Bennie Moten were there. How could I compete with people like that who were already established? Part of it, too, was that I'm a natural adventurer. And then in 1933 I had a problem with a woman. So I was real angry until I went out on the highway with my bags and this man who owned the Cherry Blossom came past. He was going for a drive, and he saw me and said, "Where you going?"

I said, "Well, I'm going as far as you go." And do you know, I convinced that man, in Kansas City, to drive me to St Louis at eight o'clock in the morning. Then I convinced him to drive me from St Louis to 39th Street and South Parkway in Chicago, by the Grand Terrace. Now that's pretty good talking, but he did it, and I guess he was glad, he was proud of it. I guess he was fascinated too. I was telling him so many yarns about how great he was, and what he should do is go to Chicago because there were a lot of chorus girls and pretty women there, and they'd come back to Kansas City with him without any hesitation whatsoever.

And he went for it. I was so embarrassed. I went in one door in this Ritz Hotel next to the Grand Terrace. I went in one door and out the other. I still remember how nice he was to me, and I think this is how life is. I hope I paid my reward for his kindness, and if I see a person in distress and I can help, I will.

So when I got to Chicago I lived in a house with a musical family – the name was Warren Smith. And I knew a lot of people. There were a lot of the great guys and you had an opportunity to hear a lot of good jazz around. They didn't all stay in the same place – they'd move around. I knew Jesse Stone: he was a fine arranger and piano player, and he had a band in one of the clubs. Budd Johnson was there. Fats was there. There was a guy named Stumpy Evans, a tenor saxophone player. Then I met Jimmie Noone and Earl Hines, Barney Bigard, Omer Simeon (who was playing the drums for Earl), Charlie Carpenter (the guy who wrote *Rosetta* with Earl), Wallace Bishop, Billy Eckstine, Tiny Parham, Dinah Washington, and May Alix (a singer). Then I began to see where the Pekin Cafe was, and heard Louis and Teddy Wilson. I could never understand how those guys could rehearse so much, 'cause I never rehearsed. I imagine that's the reason why I didn't become a classical pianist, 'cause you gotta rehearse quite a bit; you just have to devote maybe two, three hours a day to rehearse.

I went around every morning to the breakfast dance. That's just when they had a special show say at four o'clock – the places closed at four or five o'clock. They'd have music and a dance every morning at one of the different clubs, and all of the people would come. I guess it was one way that each club would have of increasing its business. One Sunday night it was at the Club DeLisa – that's where Albert Ammons was playing – and they had a big show and all that. Hundreds of people came from other clubs and tried to get in – people from the Panama Club where Nat "King" Cole used to play and people from the DeLuxe. Jimmie Noone's band, and Teddy Wilson's band, and musicians that played out on the North Side, the white spots, they all came.

And I never will forget one morning they had a breakfast dance at the Grand Terrace. Earl Hines came in with a party, and I jumped up from my table and ran over to the piano and started playing *Deep Forest*. That was his theme song. And the people thought I was crazy: "Man, don't you see Earl Hines? What are you trying to play his song for?" I only wanted to let Earl Hines know that I loved him so, that I knew his theme song. The guys made it look like I was crazy, so I had to sneak out the back door. They gave me hell, and I never mentioned that to Earl. Years later, in 1975, he and I were featured together at the Nice Festival. That's when I told him that I was the guy that played his theme, and he laughed like hell. He said, "I wondered what that foolishness was." He said, "Well, where did you go?"

I said, "Well, I went home and got under the cover, I was so embarrassed."

One thing about Earl, he never acknowledged that he knew my name, from 1933 until he died. Whenever they said, "Sam Price, meet Earl Hines," he'd meet me all over again.

Chicago was all right. I knew these people that were supposed to be gangsters. So I went down to 22nd and Wabash Road, right across from Big Jim Colisimo's, and got a job at a place called the Derby Cafe. I had Zutty Singleton and people like that working with me there. So I stayed in Chicago through the summer of 1933. There was a fair – the Century of Progress Exposition. Then I met this guy who came from Toronto. He had a return ticket to Toronto, but he didn't want to go, and he gave me the ticket. Well in those days it wasn't easy to try to get from one country to another, so I got on that train going to Toronto. When I got near the border the man asked me where I was going. I said, "I'm going back to Toronto."

He said, "You live in Toronto?"

"Yeah."

He knew I was lying. He says, "Where do you live?" I told him. He says, "Where is Simpson's store?" It was one of them big department stores – I think it was Simpson's.

My mouth was open. "Simpson's? I don't think I know where that is."

He says, "OK. You get off at the next stop."

So they put me off the train in Durand, Michigan. I called a guy and told him to send me a ticket. He sent me a ticket and I went to Detroit. I walked into town, to the Harlem Club, which was supposed to be owned by gangsters, and I asked the guy for a job. He asked me where I was from, and I said, Chicago. "Who do you know?" I called a few names, and he said, "You start work tonight." And I stayed around Detroit from 1933 to 1937. I worked around there and I had an opportunity to meet a lot of musicians.

Detroit is where I heard Chick Webb for the first time. Then I had the opportunity to see Duke Ellington close up and to see Johnny Hodges and Sonny Greer. Sonny Greer was next in line as far as popularity went. Then you had Juan Tizol, Tricky Sam Nanton, Wellman Braud, and Lawrence Brown. I knew Lawrence Brown's name from Paul Howard's Quality Serenaders in California. That's the band I think that Lionel Hampton played with, too. Although Detroit at that time was not really noted, a lot of bands came through and played the Fox Theater and the Graystone Ballroom. Later on it became noted as a "Good Big Fun Town." Shows were still the principal items, though there was this transition period from shows where they'd have, like vaudeville, and maybe the principal act would be the band.

You had guys like Lanky Bowman, Benny Pippen, and Billy Bowen. Billy came from Detroit, and he went with McKinney's Cotton Pickers. I think he was the youngest conductor they ever had. McKinney had a good band – David "Fathead" Newman and Sidney De Paris. And Don Redman, well known as a writer and a playing musician, he came from Detroit. But it wasn't until after the war that there were a lot of guys who came out of Detroit – people like Milt Jackson and Kenny Burrell.

To begin with I didn't have my own band in Detroit. I started playing with Bill Johnson, who was one of the local trumpet players. And we had this unique drummer. His name was Freddie Bryant. He could play the drums, play the violin and sing, doing all of these things simultaneously. He was almost a one-man band.

Later on I was working in a place called the Chequers Barbeque with my own group. And do you know that one night I needed a drummer, and I went to the Rhythm Club – see, musicians used to gather in certain spots in various parts of the country – and this kid was there. He had a little straw hat, and his drums in a paper bag. And I asked him his name and he said, "J. C. Heard." And from that moment on J. C. Heard became one of my protégés. He used to have a problem of rushing tempos, but he went on to become one of the all-time greats as a percussionist, to be rated along with Jo Jones and those top guys. He played with all kinds of bands – Teddy Wilson, Cab Calloway, Jazz at the Philharmonic. And I was so proud that one year I took him to this festival in Cannes, and we had Sidney Bechet, Coleman Hawkins, and Roy Eldridge, and he was the only one who received an award at this festival. It was because they only had one drummer and he had to do all of the playing. So I said to the impresario, "You got to do something special for him." And they gave him an award. To hear J. C. play with Dorothy Donegan, she was fantastic and so was he. I'd consider it and classify it as a game of skill, to have the two of them playing together as they did. I'd rate J. C. as one of the all-time greats. He was a nice guy.

Whenever I have a female problem, I always move on. Like Jimmy Shine, I will pack my clothes and move on down the line. And usually when I made those decisions it was at night, and, as a rule, I'd leave in the morning. I make overnight decisions, snap decisions. I had a problem in Detroit, a female problem, so I decided to go to New York. I left Detroit and went to Cleveland, where I stopped by to see Art Tatum and Lannie Scott, and then from there I went on to New York.

4

Recording for Decca

When I got to New York in 1937 it was something else. I used to walk out in front of 2040 Seventh Avenue and I'd see Louis Armstrong and Cab Calloway and Cootie Williams and Sonny Greer and Ivie Anderson and Mary Lou Williams all coming to New York to play the Apollo Theatre, coming to New York to make recordings, or coming to New York, passing through. And you just never knew who you'd see next. It was a thrill each time.

It was shortly after I arrived in New York that I met Mayo Williams again. I was in the Woodside Hotel and I saw Count Basie's valet Jack, who said that Mayo Williams was in town looking for somebody to play for Cow Cow Davenport. So I went and met Mayo and we renewed our acquaintance. He had told me that if I ever came to New York I should look him up. He said that Cow Cow Davenport had arthritis and couldn't play and that he was trying to find somebody that could play the blues. So I went up to see Cow Cow and he said, "Sam Price! Hey, Mayo, I got it! This kid beat me playing the piano in Norfolk, Virginia, and I liked him. I taught him *The Cow Cow Blues*." Anyway, we made *Railroad Blues, That'll get it* and other things. Most guys around New York wouldn't play a lot of those numbers, they'd only play *Carolina Shout* and all that. So after we recorded those things for Davenport Mayo said, "Listen, I'm going out to Chicago to get Roosevelt Sykes. You wanna ride with me?" And from that day on I was with Decca as house pianist and recording supervisor.

Mayo and I brought Jimmie Gordon from Chicago, and the first thing I did was to play piano for him. Teddy Bunn and Richard Fullbright, who had been on the session with Davenport, were there too. Can you imagine me having arrived in New York City, being in the same town as Duke Ellington, Count Basie and all those great people, and going down to Decca, the same company that the sweet-music king Guy Lombardo and Bing Crosby were with, and making a hundred dollars for a day's work? I had a car, a whole lot of money, and to earn it I did all kinds of things for Decca. Mayo used to call me up and say, "Come on down here. I want you to listen to this singer." You wouldn't believe how many lousy singers he'd have me sit and listen to. Decca used to get them out of the woodwork. One time they called me and said, "Guy Lombardo thinks his piano is out of tune. Would you look at it?"

I said, "Sure," and checked it out. I really didn't find anything wrong with it, but I didn't want to get on Guy's bad side by saying that, so I said, "Well, this key here is a little off," and everybody was happy.

The Decca studios were at 50 West 57th Street, on the ninth floor. We used to record with separate microphones for the voice and instruments – just one for the whole group. It changed a little while I was there as they began to improve all their equipment. But I think that Decca was probably the last record company to transfer over to having a lot of microphones and all that stuff. They were still recording in a very simple way and making good records.

This would be my schedule. If I had a recording date it would be from 9 a.m. to 12. Then I'd go back home, eat breakfast and go back to bed. I'd wake up at six and go out to Mrs Frazier's restaurant and eat, then maybe go down Broadway to a show or go to a play, and after that go to work at, say, ten o'clock. If I wasn't working anywhere I'd hang around with some of the Cotton Club girls or at the Zanzibar, the Ubangi or Smalls' Paradise, and after leaving there I'd go to some after-hours joint. Each club would have a breakfast show. If I happened to go to Monroe's Uptown House I'd see many celebrities – people like Mickey Rooney or Cary Grant, Art Tatum, Billie Holiday, John Hammond, Canada Lee – each one surrounded by worshipers. Then, about four o'clock, I'd go to bed.

On Thursday nights I didn't go to bed. On Thursdays I

went straight through that routine, but at eight o'clock I'd go to somebody's apartment or someplace like that and drink, and wait for the Apollo Theatre to open for the first show, because at that first show you'd get more entertainment. Usually the show would end up too long, so they'd have to cut it down. And Friday morning was the opening day. And oh, the hustle and bustle, and guys pushing, and long lines to get a seat. Fans wanting to hear Johnny Hodges's new solo on *Mood Indigo,* or whatever it was. Everybody was there for Duke's opening because the band was so delicate, so rare, so fabulous.

I played with a whole bunch of singers for Decca – Trixie Smith, Coot Grant and Wesley Wilson, Blue Lu Barker, Johnnie Temple, Peetie Wheatstraw. Peetie Wheatstraw also recorded under the names the Devil's Son-in-Law and the High Sheriff from Hell. His real name was William Bunch, and he played the guitar. What happened with a lot of these musicians was that they could only play in one key. They'd go into the studio and want to play songs in E natural, guitar keys like that, and the other musicians couldn't play with them. But what I would do was take a song to the closest key that a musician could play in to make it a little easier. And I did that for many of the singers. Singers like Georgia White. She would always sing in a key that was too high, then louse it up, go out of range and get laryngitis. I'd find her key, drop it down and keep it in the right range for her voice.

I did a few sessions with Blue Lu Barker. I was the contractor all the time, so I booked the musicians. I'd get the best musicians available, like Chu Berry, Lester Young – any guy like that. Her song *Don't you make me high* – they tried to ban it. Some people liked it, some people thought it was funny, some thought it was suggestive, you know. It could actually have been banned in places like Alabama and Georgia – places like that. I read in Paul Oliver's book that they had a sign in Alabama, directed at white people, that said "Don't let your children listen to this nigger music." But I never did believe in suggestive stuff. Guys like Peetie Wheatstraw and Johnnie Temple, they'd just write songs like

Big Legged Susie – things like that – and they were considered race records. And Decca would record them and the people would buy them.

I recorded with Ollie Shepard too. He was a piano player, but I played piano on a session with him in April 1939 because he wasn't in the union, and that meant he couldn't play with other musicians. Sometimes I'd end up playing for a guy in the studio because he'd get drunk or he would just get stage fright.

Eventually I talked Decca into giving me my own session – Sam Price and his Texas Blusicians. This was 13 March 1940. I just picked up a bunch of musicians for that session – Don Stovall and all those guys – and we made *Fetch it to me* and and instrumental version of *Cow Cow Blues*. It was my arrangement that I recorded, and later Bob Crosby took the whole arrangement, note for note, and didn't say a word to me. Well, I didn't care, because I wasn't greedy and I was making money and I had gained recognition. We also made *Swinging out in the Groove*, which was my first vocal on record.

Later that year, in another session, I sang a song called *Thinking*. I had no idea that the damn song was anything, but people were writing me letters. I wanted to, but I never really could sing; it's one of the things I never could bring myself to do. I did this thing *Just Jivin' Around* with Lester Young – I thought it was a great record. And in the same session we did a tune with Yack Taylor, *Things 'bout coming my way*, which was a blues. She was singing it awful, but Lester was playing good.

I did a lot of stuff also with gospel singers, Sister Rosetta Tharpe and so on. Earlier on I told you that I came from a long line of religious singers, and you could be banished from the clan if you sang gospel songs or if you sang songs with too much rhythm and that sort of thing – although back in those days the Church of God in Christ people were doing it in the Church. So one day Milt Gabler asked Mayo to have me come down to see him. A guy had written a song called *Two Little Fishes and Five Loaves of Bread*. It wasn't really a gospel song, but it was about the Lord taking the fishes and what he did with them and all. So he asked me, would I consider recording with Rosetta Tharpe. Well, you know Rosetta Tharpe tuned her guitar funny and sang in the wrong key, and the meter sometimes wasn't exact. She could sing and all that, but then she was a folksinger, more or less. So I told Mayo I'd have to think about it.

And they sent Rosetta Tharpe's mother to see me and to explain to me that if, when a song was played, the thinking behind it was right, then there was nothing wrong with it. I knew I wasn't going to play anything but the blues, anyway – blues, boogie-woogie, mix it up and play jazz – but in a religious vein. I was reluctant, but money will change your mind, and finally I said, "OK, let's try."

Jack and Dave Kapp and Mayo and me, we had this big conference, because they were wondering what to do with her (she'd worked with Millinder with all those horns behind her), and Jack, the president of Decca, asked me, "Sam, what can we do with her?" They used to ask me about artists, how to feature them, because they weren't trained musicians. I knew more about their music and how to present it because, although I wasn't trained, I'd had more practice; I could play with them. So I would tell them what to do. And with Rosetta, I'd tell her how to move her capo and get the guitar in the right key, because without the capo she'd sing in A and E, all those guitar keys. With a capo on the fret it would be a better key to play along with, a normal jazz key. And I gave her a better background, not so fancy – just simple. I played plain boogie-woogie on a lot of songs, or slow blues in a gospel vein.

So one of the first things we made was *Two Little Fishes and Five Loaves of Bread* and it was a big hit. But she didn't want to pay me the royalties. So I said, "OK, you come to town, get the songs and bring them to me. I'll do ten songs for you for $1000. I'll work three days a week with you and straighten your songs out. I'll hire the musicians and you just pay them union scale. I'll take care of everything – you don't have to worry." Rosetta used to want me to make the records, and she'd give me the $1000, reluctantly. But then she'd go and get another piano player to go out on the road, and she'd call him Sam Price, and say "Sam Price and his Trio." One time she went into my home town with this guy, Jimmy Roost – a yellow dude, a real albino-looking cat. She went into my home town with that shit and they rode her out so fast. All my relatives were there in the audience, and she'd say, "And now, my piano player, Sam Price," and here comes this light boy.

Five or six times I made that $1000 working with Rosetta, and I used good jazz musicians – Billy Taylor, Wallace Bishop, Pops Foster, Kenny Clarke. I think that was one of the things that made the records a hit. Rosetta Tharpe never gave me a Christmas card, and I made her a lot of money. But that is the thing about my piano playing: if my piano can benefit somebody, I'm not jealous.

And then there was Cousin Joe. He wasn't no blues singer, but he could write words very well. Danny Barker said he was his cousin. I was down at Decca, so I told Mayo there was this dude in town that could write good lyrics. He wrote *Box Car Shorty* and *Begging Woman*. Then I got Mezz Mezzrow to record him. I try to see something in a guy. Somebody said Cousin Joe tried to play piano when he went back to New Orleans. On the records with me he was just singing. That's his forte – that and writing.

The first time I played behind Ella Fitzgerald I became very confused, very frightened. We were doing a cover version of a song, *Do I worry*, during that strike – that recording ban. They tried to match some male singers behind her and all, and it didn't work. I didn't have confidence because I wasn't doing it my way. She had the same simple approach if you knew how to handle it the right way, but they were trying to dress it up too complicated. But at Decca they let me do it my way; I got it right. And they made a lot of money and I made a lot of money. I spent a lot of it at the racetrack. I used to go down to Decca at nine o'clock in the morning, and by one o'clock I could be at the racetrack. I did that all through the years I was there. But the thing I liked about Decca was that they were nice to me; I was on the staff and I had an office and all that.

I stopped working for Decca in 1954. It was then, because I went down to Dallas and didn't come back to New York for a while. One of the last records I recall making was with Sy Oliver for Sister Rosetta Tharpe, and he thought he could do the arrangements for the musical background and all much better than myself. But I think his arrangements were a little too thick – not like his Lunceford arrangements, which I think were more difficult than dense. He thought he could transform Rosetta Tharpe's style. He had Marlowe Morris on organ and it just destroyed the purity – the essence of the thing. See, me and the trio were very simple, very clean.

So in New York, apart from all the record dates, I worked at the clubs. The first job I got was with Hot Lips Page. My uncle told me not to buy a tuxedo, that he had one, and he put it in the cleaners for me. So I got the tuxedo and headed for my job, and when I got down to 42nd Street I felt a little funny. But I said to myself that things would be all right, and I went to dinner with some chicks from the Cotton Club and headed back for my first night with Lips. We all had dressing rooms, so I went up, had a shower and started to change – new patent leather shoes, a new dress shirt, clean socks and underwear. Finally I put on the pants and found the legs were too short. I had one hell of a time getting into them. When Lips said, "All on," I came out of the room and everybody started to laugh. Lips called me Prince Whistle Britches and, to add injury to insult, when I sat down the pants busted and we all had a big laugh.

In the early 1950s I played at the Cafe Society Downtown, where Kenny Kersey and Cliff Jackson, Billie Holiday, Hazel Scott, and Lena Horne were all together, and it was quite a showcase and a nice place to work. You could get a complete dinner there back in the 1940s for a dollar fifty cents. At the Cafe Society I always picked the guys. They had to have two things – they had to be able to play well and they had to have a good reputation. You see, I'm keen on publicity. We used to get a lot of famous people in – people like Toscanini,

Henry Fonda, Canada Lee, Paul Robeson, Zero Mostel, Jackie Gifford, Imogene Coca. They used to come in to hear Art Tatum. The Cafe Society Downtown was the first integrated nightclub in America; the audience was mixed, and there was no problem to get in. All you had to do was try to make a reservation, because the place was so popular.

We had a man in Harlem at one time, name of Oscar Hammerstein, who was like an official host. When people were coming to New York they would phone Oscar and say, "Listen, we'll be in town Thursday through Sunday. Make plans for us." What he would do would be to make reservations for the Cafe Society, and always ringside. Every place he took you, it was ringside – wasn't no sitting behind a post with Oscar. He became quite an official host, an official greeter for the city, especially with Blacks, because some places were kind of funny – sit you behind posts and all that.

Some places on 52nd Street were kind of funny too – like Leon and Eddie's and the 21 Club, I think it was called. You just didn't go in there. You didn't even go that way on 52nd Street – the buck stopped in the middle of the block, west of Sixth Avenue. But, like Jimmy Ryan's, it wasn't lily white, 'cause they had black musicians playing there and occasionally black people went in. And even the Theresa Hotel. A black person couldn't get a room in the Theresa not long before that. And you'd go in some places and they'd give you a Mickey Finn. They were kind of funny in Jack Dempsey's. I was in there once with Tallulah Bankhead and I noticed the man's sleeve in the soup and a few other things – I was up to a lot of their tricks. So I asked for the check and I gave a thousand-dollar bill, and I ran his ass all over Broadway trying to get that thing changed.

Tallulah was quite a jazz fan and she was one of my staunch supporters. She liked blues and she liked jazz, and she loved Sidney Bechet. This is how I got to play in her show *Clash by Night*. What happened was that Billy Rose called Barney Josephson and asked him to have me come up to the Diamond Horseshoe. What they wanted was a blues, not quite like *Rhapsody in Blue*, but more a blues mood, sad and tragic – lonesome music. Billy Rose wasn't at the Diamond Horseshoe, but he asked me to come over to his house on Sutton Place. I went over and he said, "Sam, now I'll tell you. I don't care what happens, you got the job." He wanted two piano players. "You got one of the jobs. Don't worry." Do you know, he called at least a hundred piano players to play with me? But what he wanted, primarily, was a guy that could read some little notes and cues, that's what he wanted. He also wanted an untrained piano player; he wanted the sound to be primitive, and this is what I was playing. But he wanted the other piano player to be able to play with me, so it would show a contrast but it would work together. So we tried everybody – James P. Johnson, Willie "the Lion" Smith, Donald Lambert, Meade "Lux" Lewis, Pete Johnson. I thought James P. was going to get it – I thought they were going to go by the name of the person – but they finally ended up selecting Arthur Gibbs, the man that wrote that song *Running Wild*.

Now, we rehearsed this show, we tried out in Detroit and we played in Philadelphia. One day in New York, when we were getting ready to open, Tallulah Bankhead went up on the right side of the theater. There was one scene where you could not see her for a fleeting moment – she would disappear from view. And she said to Billy, "Billy, I'm lost." Then she recited some lines before she came back into view. Anyway, she told him to change that and he wouldn't, so she barred him from the theater. She said, "If you come in here, I'm not doing the show." And he had to stay away, so the show finally closed. It later became a very successful movie, but I don't think they carried out the idea about the music. The whole thing was just the kind of triplets, thirds and tremolo you get in something like *Freight Train Blues*.

After the show closed I went back to the Cafe Society, but one night there was a free-for-all fight in the club, and the place had to close. Then I went out to Flatbush Avenue in Brooklyn to open a club called Max the Mayor. Max didn't understand how to keep an account of his stock, so I had to

Sammy aged 15

Sammy and Bob with their uncle Joseph E. Ford

Sammy's brother Robert (Bob)

Sammy with Art Tatum and Teddy Wilson, 1938

Joe Brown's band, 1939: Frank "Coco" Darling (double bass), unknown (drums), Sammy, Joe Brown (trumpet)

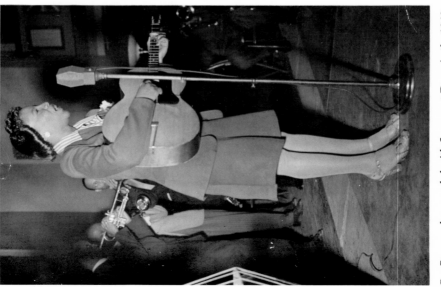

Bea Booze, who recorded with Sammy at Decca in the 1940s

Sammy with Sister Rosetta Tharpe (left) and Marie Knight

Sammy with Muggsy Spanier, Kansas Fields, Ike Levy (founder of CBS) and James P. Johnson

Poster for the first concert given by the Philadelphia Jazz Society (1946)

Philadelphia, 15 September 1946: Baby Dodds, Sidney Bechet, Mezz Mezzrow, George Lugg, Jack Butler

Sammy at Club Logan, Philadelphia, to promote the Philadelphia Jazz Society, (left to right): Senor Chapotine, Benny Morton, unknown, Oscar Sadler, Bill Coleman, unknown, Charles Green, Ed Hall, Felix Valdero, unknown, unknown

Lester Young, Mezz Mezzrow and Frankie Newton playing at one of Sammy's Philadelphia Jazz Festival concerts

Philadelphia: Sammy with George Baquet and Bunk Johnson

Philadelphia: Sammy with Pee Wee Russell, Jack Lesberg, Max Kaminsky, Fred Ohms and Bud Freeman

Philadelphia: Mezz Mezzrow, Sidney Bechet, Danny Alvin (playing George Wettling's drum kit) and Wild Bill Davison; Sammy is behind Mezzrow

Sammy playing at Jimmy Ryan's, New York, late 1940s (left to right): Bertha "Chippie" Hill, Don Frye, unknown, Sidney Bechet, Big Chief Russell Moore, unknown, unknown, Bob Wilber, unknown

Sammy and Pops Foster; photograph signed by musicians and friends at the Nice Jazz Festival, 1948

Louis Armstrong's All Stars at the Nice Jazz Festival, 1948: Sid Catlett, Jack Teagarden, Armstrong, Barney Bigard, Arvell Shaw, Velma Middleton

Sammy: le sorcier

Marseilles, 1948 (after the Nice Jazz Festival): personnel includes Mezz Mezzrow, Dizzy Gillespie, Sammy and Arvell Shaw

Children's egg-roll organized by Sammy and the People's Funeral Home, Dallas, 1954

Baby Dodds, Philadelphia, 1946

Pops Foster, Paris, 1956

Publicity shot of Sammy Price and his All Stars in Europe, 1956 (left to right): Herb Hall, Emmett Berry, Pops Foster, Freddie Moore, George Stevenson

The band in France: personnel includes Herb Hall, Emmett Berry, George Stevenson and Pops Foster

On stage in Paris (left to right): Sammy, Emmett Berry, Herb Hall, Freddie Moore, Pops Foster and George Stevenson

Sammy with wife Nancy and daughter Sharon read the news

Herb Hall, Pops Foster and Sammy discuss the merits of Abdul's carpet, Tunis, 1956

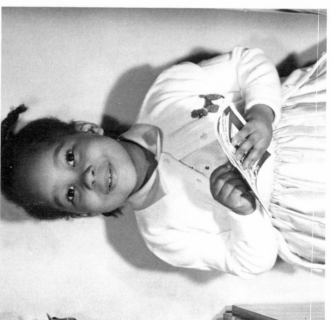

Sammy's daughter Sharon signing autographs in France, 1956

Sammy conducting the Sidney Bechet memorial concert, Carnegie Hall, 1959

At the Sidney Bechet memorial concert (left to right): Sol Yaged, Gene Sedric, Bennie Moten, Hal Singer, Garvin Bushell, Paul Quinichette, Cecil Scott, Herb Hall and Bob Wilber

Sammy at the Metropole, New York, with Henry "Red" Allen, Rufus "Speedy" Jones, Buster Bailey and Herb Flemming

J. C. Higginbotham, Buster Bailey, Sammy and Herb Flemming help Red Allen celebrate his fifth anniversary at the Metropole, 1958

Sammy with (left to right): Louis Armstrong, Henry "Red" Allen and Lucille Armstrong, 1960

Sammy with his mother, his wife and the French Consul General, New York, 1960s

Sammy in his office at 126th Street and Seventh Avenue, New York, 1975

Sammy's 69th birthday celebrations at the Crawdaddy, Roosevelt Hotel, New York, 1977 (left to right): Monty Irvine, Eubie Blake, "The King of Boogie-Woogie" and Mr D. Straub, hotel executive

Sammy with (left to right): Janice Davis, his daughters Sharon Mack and Mary Bonelli, and his grand-daughter Brenda Bonelli

Sammy with Mayor Koch

Sammy at the Copley Plaza Hotel, Boston, with Paula Elliott

Sammy with William Heck, vice-president of the Copley Plaza, and Lawrence Bethune, dean of students at the Berklee College of Music

Sammy at Simmons College, 1986

Sammy with Buck Clayton, 1984

show him and his partner how to take an inventory on their whiskey. The bartender just poured the bottle until it was empty, then they'd take all of the empty bottles and put them in the back and set full ones back on the bar. So I showed them: "Hey, Max. Look man, how many bottles of whiskey you got? Twenty? OK. How many you putting out on the bar? Twenty? OK. Put ten in reserve, then check on the bottles, see what's left and estimate the amount of whiskey still in each bottle." And then I had the band. I had Cecil Scott, Ben Webster, Henry "Red" Allen, J. C. Heard, and dozens of great musicians, and the place became real popular.

5

Festivals, Philadelphia and France

During the time I was working for Decca I had an office at 1674 Broadway. I had a license as a booking agent – a legitimate booking agent, not sub-booking for somebody – which my uncle Joe helped me to get. I also had a piano there where Willie "the Lion" Smith and James P. Johnson used to come and practice, which I did just out of respect for them. My uncle, who was around in central Harlem, was called Joseph E. Ford. And, aside from having all these other good things happen to me – getting jobs and making records and broadening my acquaintance with a lot of people – this is how I found my uncle Joe. There was an NAACP boat ride, and this man was standing down at 125th Street on the pier selling tickets for this boat ride. I had eight people with me, and I walked up to him and I recognized him – I hadn't seen him since 1913. And he was saying, "Tickets?"

And I said, "Yes, I want nine tickets. I've been looking for you."

And I guess he thought I was the FBI or something. So he said, "What did I do now?"

I said, "Do you know who I am? I'm your sister's son." He was a dark man, but for a moment he turned snow white. He was flabbergasted when he found out who I was and that it was real. It took me a moment to say, "Well now, your father's name was Elbert and your mother's name was Mary Jane." And then I started acquainting him with the past and we had a big reunion. And on the boat I met Adam Clayton Powell, and that was my introduction to the political arena. Uncle Joe managed Powell's political affairs.

Around this time I was approached by James P. Johnson's people to help with a concert they were having in Carnegie

Hall to play his piece *Yamekraw*. There was a problem they had in getting enough money to prepare the score, and I was helping there. But the tragedy of the thing was that the day we were having the concert, in 1945, was the day that President Roosevelt died, and the world stood still. So it meant that we had to postpone the thing for a week, and after that the same enthusiasm wasn't there. As a result I don't think we made a profit. But then James P. and I became very close, because he knew that I was proud of him as a man and an artist, and he was grateful to me for that until his death. I think the reason he didn't have success with his works was that the Broadway promoters forgot that here was a man that wrote the song *The Charleston*. He should have been able to find financial support for anything he wanted to do.

I was one of the first black people in America to do a jazz festival or festival concerts. Al Rose, who was a disc jockey in Philadelphia, had the idea to have some jazz sessions, and he approached me, along with Miss Jane Bowman and a lawyer. They said, "Well, we're interested in doing something in jazz, but we can't be interested in the thing to underwrite it." I felt like in order for it to be a success you'd have to have these sessions every week. So we got together and organized the Jazz Festival Society of Philadelphia, and we had these sessions – regular concerts – every Sunday afternoon. I lived in New York and commuted to Philadelphia.

And then I bought a club with a guy called Felix Valdez, and we used to have Jazz Festival Society concerts in the club. It was a private social club, where you could bring your own bottle. This was good for us, because many of our members were minors. There was a blue law in Philadelphia, and you couldn't buy whiskey on a Sunday. Then I went to Ike Levy and asked him to call the Academy of Music and see if they'd let me have the foyer, a small hall holding about 250 people. Mr Mason was the manager of the Academy. Ike called him, and he said, "Yes." So then I started having the concerts in the foyer of the Academy of Music. What happened was that you joined the society and you paid two or three dollars for to come in and hear the music. You didn't *have* to join – because I was practical and wanted to sell tickets. All you had to have, to come into the concert, was the money for the ticket.

I had a lot of tiffs with guys in Philadelphia who tried to tell me who to hire, and I would just tell them, "Well, it's my money." I had people like Mezzrow, Pee Wee Russell, Max Kaminsky, Jimmy Archey, Pops Foster, and Baby Dodds to play there. I hired Bunk Johnson. That's when that photograph with George Baquet was taken. Bunk had staged a comeback then and was much better. I'd try to hire guys who would sound good together. I had pretty good judgement about who to hire and who would sound good together. I had Mezz every week. He wasn't as popular as he was reliable. Because, you see, I brought the guys from New York, and I would depend on Mezz to get the tickets, meet the guys at the station at 12 o'clock and get to Philadelphia by one. He'd do that. And I'd call the guys and say, "Mezz'll have your ticket. Be at the station."

One time we decided to have a battle of tenor saxophones. We had Lester Young and Zack Wright and Jimmy Oliver. Oliver was the local rage. This was on a Sunday at Town Hall in Philadelphia, and, I'm telling you, I came up in a cab and I saw lots of cars and all of these people coming up out of the subway in big crowds and I said, "What on earth is happening? Maybe they had an accident or something." When I got to Town Hall it was packed to the rafters, and we had a very, very successful concert.

Then I also had a big festival, in another hall, as a special promotion. That's when I had Art Tatum and Sidney Bechet. I say that that was the first jazz festival ever held in America by a black man; I don't remember anybody else having held one before 1947. It cost me over a thousand dollars, which I had to pay out. Art Tatum had promised that he'd play, and that if I lost money he'd give me some of the money back. But Joe Marsala, his manager, vetoed that. Anyway, we had about three or four thousand people and the concert was a big hit.

My only problem with the organization was that I had no conception about money. If our net profit was $300 after we'd paid everybody and all expenses, I'd take the $300 and entertain the musicians with it, take them to a restaurant and have a big feast. I never really made a profit out of any of those concerts. I discontinued them in 1947 because there was a guy in Philadelphia who started having jazz in a club every night. And then sometimes some of the musicians didn't turn up, and this would create a problem for the society, who would get the blame. But I had a pretty good stay in Philadelphia.

While I was there the Strand Ballroom was run by Reese Dupree. We had a concert, Reese and I. We had Ella Fitzgerald and Cootie Williams's band. And after the concert Reese had a bunch of guys with him who were real tough. He had taken all the money and put it in a bag, then sat down with the bag under his chair, and these guys were standing around him with guns. And I said, "Well, Reese, let's check up."

He said, "Price, I just can't help it."

I said, "Can't help what?" He started telling me what he owed. I said, "OK."

I went to Albert Greenfield, who owned the Strand Ballroom building, and I entered into a tentative agreement to buy the building where the ballroom was operating. I got possession and evicted Reese Dupree. Then I changed the name of the building to Price's Palace. That's a matter of history, and can be corroborated. Well, I knew I couldn't hold onto it. How could you have a building with a dance hall that's dark six days a week because there were no attractions and then only an occasional dance?

Before all this, in 1945, I did some recording sessions with Mezz. He had found somebody with money, and he came to me – I don't know why people always come to me when they have money – and he asked me if I'd like to do some recordings. I did all of those tunes for Mezz on the King Jazz label. I did *133rd Street Boogie*, *Step down, step up*, and things like that. That was the first solo session, which we did in New York; I think it was at Nola's Studio on Broadway. We also did some things with a seven-piece band – things like *House Party* and *Revolutionary Blues* – with Lips Page, Sidney Bechet, Mezz, myself, Danny Barker, Pops Foster and Sid Catlett. Lips did some singing. Then we did a second session in Chicago in 1947. We had a five-piece band for that. Kaiser Marshall was on drums. I'm sure I was supposed to get a composer's royalty for those sessions. Mezz took the masters to some guys, and I understand they took the tapes away from him, and they just disappeared.

Mezz and I became friends, very good friends. I never judge a man by his skin. As long as he treats me all right and he's courteous to my friends I accept him. I gave Mezz every respect in Philadelphia. I paid him 50 bucks every Sunday afternoon. It was unfortunate that he got involved in problems early in his life, but he had a heart as good as gold. There was one incident I remember later, when I was in France in 1956 giving concerts for the Jeunesses Musicales. The American Embassy had invited me to come to the ambassador's residence in Paris because I had been nice to the youth of France, and they recognized that. At the same time we were having that racial situation here in the South – I think it was Mississippi – with Artheline Lucy. And Mezz didn't want me to go. He said, "How can you go to the American Embassy when they're doing this to a black person?"

And I told him, "Well, one thing has nothing to do with the other. I think it's an honor for me to be invited to come to the American Embassy. The only reason I'd not go is if I had a stroke and died. When my government respects me enough to honor me with a visit to them, then they're sure that I'm carrying some kind of prestige. And then, maybe my going there will help change the situation." You see, I'm like a doctor, a repair man; I always try to repair things.

Sidney Bechet was there, and Bill Coleman and his wife, and Jack Dimitri, Kurt Mohr and Charles Delaunay. They were all there because this was a pretty big thing for American jazz musicians. Sidney felt I should go, too, and he and Mezz almost had a fight. So Mezz was pretty keen on what he believed in. I respected him for that. That was his choice.

I think Mezz was one white man who wanted to be black. He said that in his book *Really the Blues*. I can understand it. He wanted to be black, but he wasn't, he was a white man. I told him quite frankly, not to insult him, I said, "Mezz, I'm what you want to be. I'm a black man. You want to be one, but there ain't a damn thing you can do to make yourself be one but be born again." He married a black woman and had kids by this black woman, but he just wasn't a black man. And when a person is thinking a certain way, you gotta be careful that people don't misunderstand. You think he's just sitting there because he's a white man trying to be nice to black folks, but that's not really the way it is. Mezz was a nice guy, and he proved that he was faithful, but a lot of people misunderstood him.

People had divided opinions about Mezzrow as a musician. Some guy walked in to Jimmy Ryan's one night and said, "You know what? Milton Mezzrow's the only guy I know could make a clarinet sound like it's got hay fever. I once heard him before the days of long solos, before Coltrane. I think he was playing *Black and Blue*, and he played 15 minutes. I'd never heard anybody play that long before. *Black and Blue* became red and pink." But he was a good old boy.

Sidney Bechet was a very, very sensitive man, period. The shooting incident in Paris and all that – he was just ready when you were. He'd give you a chance to act swiftly, but then he'd fight back – he'd reply. I got along good with him, too. I managed his business for him. A lot of those guys relied on me for business. They acted like I was a lawyer. People like Sidney would come to me with a contract and say, "Look at this. What shall I do?" He'd ask my advice. He was living at St Nicholas Avenue then, in the early 1940s. And I used to look at the contract and say, "No good. Blah, blah, blah. You gotta do this, you gotta do that." People still come to me and ask me for assistance – you know, people getting evicted, people who can't get no heat nor hot water.

Sidney was also sensitive as a musician. When you've been around a guy and you know what he's gonna do, you can't anticipate what he's gonna do, but you know anything he's gonna do, he's spectacular. That's how I felt about Sidney. And I think he liked the sort of tone and feeling that I gave. The rhythm section for those King Jazz things with Pops Foster and Kaiser Marshall was very robust. I never did any concerts with Sidney – just recordings. Later he made some records just to do me a favor. He wanted to show me that he really appreciated me as a friend. That was for Charles Delaunay in 1956.

Sidney had two wives, you know, when he was in Paris. At the same time. He'd eat dinner with one. He'd take me, and we'd go and have dinner. Then we'd go up to the other wife and have the dessert.

When I went to France the first time, for the Nice Jazz Festival in 1948, it was by accident. Panassié wanted Willie "the Lion" Smith to go, but he couldn't make it. Mezz was organizing the thing in the States and he asked me to substitute for him. He didn't let Panassié know because in those days communication was so slow. You could write a letter today and you could get an answer next month, so whenever you got the answer it would be too late to do whatever you wanted to do. So he simply switched Willie "the Lion" Smith's ticket over to me, and I went in his stead.

There were several bands going for that international festival in Nice. I went on the same plane as Louis, Earl Hines, Jack Teagarden, Sid Catlett, Barney Bigard, Arvell Shaw, and Velma Middleton. When we got on the plane in New York at LaGuardia Airport the exhaust had a flame coming out of it. I don't know what it was, but you could see it. Earl Hines was frozen all the way just watching that flame. He thought the plane was on fire. We had a big laugh about that.

We were supposed to fly to Nice, but we couldn't land because of the weather conditions. We had to go all the way back to Orly Airport in Paris and land there. Panassié wanted to know if everybody had arrived OK. They said,

"No, Willie 'the Lion' didn't come." Panassié asked who Mezz had replaced him with, but the phone connection was bad and he couldn't understand what they were saying. The producer was yelling and Panassié was yelling: "Pappy Rice?" . . . "Who?" He didn't know what name it was. So finally it dawned on Panassié that they were saying "Sammy Price," and he said, "Oh, marvelous."

The following year Leadbelly died in New York. We were friends from the first time that I saw him, and I always treasure his friendship. He was a plain, simple man, but he was a man. When I got the call that he was dead I wasn't in the city, but I cut my trip short and returned in time for a memorial they were having at Town Hall. Whoever planned the program hung his guitar on the stage curtain and told me to stand under the guitar. When they lit up the stage I was supposed to be singing *Take this hammer and give it to the captain*. I didn't know the song, but I made up some words and got by.

It was a short time after Leadbelly's death that I went back to Dallas. There was a problem here in New York and it would have been a question of some litigation, so a lawyer decided that perhaps I should not be around in New York for a while. So I went to Montreal, and from Montreal I went to Dallas. A friend of mine there that was in the undertaking business owned a club and I suggested to him, "Why not put a piano in this club?" So he put a piano in his club and I stayed there for a while.

The guy's funeral parlor was like a graveyard. It wasn't a funeral parlor - he wasn't doing any business. People were being buried by other undertakers. So I said to him, "I'll come over to your funeral parlor and I'll start doing the public relations." Well, I always try to do something different from everybody else. When the white people were buried they always had a police motor-cycle escort, but when a black person was buried they'd just go on down the road without all that. So the first body we got, I arranged for him to have a motor-cycle escort. And everybody said, "Oh, man!"

So the next thing I did was I told him that we would have a new special funeral car to come and park in front of the funeral parlor. And we attracted all the attention in Dallas. And one guy that I knew said, "Man, I'd like to be buried in that." And two weeks later he died, and we got his body. So then it got so that this friend of mine gave me a piece of the business and I would do all the publicity for him. I would ride in a black car behind the funeral, with a motor-cycle in front. And if there was some problem I'd just cut out of the procession and straighten it out. It was a community service. And I would cry with a person when somebody died – I'd go and cry right with them. We cried till we got the insurance policy actually. The insurance policy used to take a long time to come through, and if they had any immediate problems I'd go and take care of it.

Another thing I did around that time was promote some concerts. All along this period you had singing groups, like the Ink Spots, that were becoming famous. Well, I presented the Five Blind Boys, the Soul Stirrers and the Pilgrim Travelers. And I was one of the first to present Sam Cooke with a group. And, again, all of these people came to the concert in Dallas; I thought there was another automobile wreck! You know, when you're a promoter and the recipient of something good, it's a strange feeling. Sometimes you ask yourself, "What did I do to deserve this?" Here are 3000 people coming – walking, running, in cabs, in buses – coming out to hear these singing groups. You promote something that you believe in and you find out that you can convince other people to believe in it too.

Well, another of the things I gained in Dallas was a wife. I married Nancy in 1952, and we had our little daughter Sharon. One Eastertime I gave this little egg-roll thing for the children at the house of the president of the funeral parlor. There's a photograph of the occasion, where I'm holding Sharon. Shortly after, in 1954, I decided that I'd had it with Dallas. I'd been involved with the undertaking business, I'd operated two nightclubs, and I'd played a long residency at Cain's Hitching post, but I'd got in a rut, you see, and I was longing for New York and other places. All my friends would come through on the road shows and ask, "Man, what are you doing here wasting your time?" So finally I came back to New York.

I did some more record dates back in New York. I recorded with Jimmy Rushing and I made a record for Jazztone with Jonah Jones, Pete Brown, Vic Dickenson, Cozy Cole and Milt Hinton. And the next thing I knew, somebody was calling me, wanting me to go to Europe. That was 1955, and the tour I made was booked by the impresario Jacob Levy. It was for the Jeunesses Musicales de France, an arts organization underwritten by the French government. I was told that when they booked me it was the first time they had ever booked a jazz group. It had always been classical until then. We played in the Salle Gaveau in Paris, which was an exclusive classical stronghold. We played at the Palais Chaillot, a huge auditorium, and the Olympia and the Salle Pleyel. And we made a lot of records. We enjoyed a very, very big success. I didn't get a lot of money, though: I guess that money and opportunity just don't go together.

In the band I had Emmett Berry, George Stevenson, Herbie Hall, Pops Foster and Fred Moore. We toured all over France and we also went to North Africa – to Tunisia and Algiers. There was no club work, only concerts: I think we did 46 concerts. There was a reception prior to every concert. The people were so very nice to us, but we used to run from giving autographs. But then I thought, "Hey, this is silly. This is the way you become popular." So what we would do, because Freddie Moore couldn't write too fast, if we thought a thousand people were gonna be there, was autograph a thousand signatures beforehand. We had this promotional postcard which we gave out at concerts, and we'd autograph that.

We were doing all these concerts, and Sharon was sitting in the audience with my wife. One night Sharon asked me, "Daddy, can I come up where you are on the stage?" And I let her come up on the stage. At the end we always played *When the saints go marching in*, and we would parade around.

So I had an idea that when we would parade I'd let her come up among the band. The last person would be the trombonist, George Stevenson, and I'd have Sharon prancing along with the flag. And as a result of that, the next day when the paper came out they had three pictures of Sharon and nothing about me! So then I kept that in, and I paid her 25 francs a night.

There's a picture of Sharon signing autographs on that French tour. She said, "Well, Daddy, let me change my clothes before you give out any autographs." And I had to wait until she'd changed. And she couldn't write – she'd just scratch her "name" on the paper. When we got back to Paris I said, "Well, we're going home tomorrow."

She said, "How many days do we travel?"

I said, "Five days."

She said, "How much do I get?"

I said, "Well, Sharon, your job is over."

She said, "Oh, no. It ain't my business if you don't have a job for me. You got to pay me." So I had to pay her, and I always put her money under the pillow, so when she woke up it would be under there.

The other guys all liked that trip. I was giving them a good salary – that would make you like it. Of course I didn't like the conduct of some of them. They used to get high. One night I played them a dirty trick; I punished them. When we first got to France they didn't even know how to ask for the door key or what room they were in. And one night one of the fellows just took a bottle of whiskey and drank it down before we played. So I said, "I'll get him." So all I had to do was go get in the bus, and when the bus stopped, while they were getting out, I was in to the concierge, got my key and was upstairs, and I locked the door and put the lights out. Now they had to stay out of their rooms all night, 'cause they didn't know how to say "key" or "room," and they was knockin' on my door for me to tell them. But I just didn't even answer. So that taught them a lesson. But they were never straight. I had a lot of hardships with some of those guys. George Stevenson would lure another member of the band off and they'd drink that whiskey before they'd start playing. That was very distracting to me, because I wanted the best for the young people to see.

I worked a lot with Pops Foster, apart from that tour. He was great. He was one of my bass players back in Philadelphia, for the Festival Society. I look for clarity in a bass player; I'm keen on the sound of the instrument. I may play bad myself, but you can always hear it well. And I try to match musicians. Nobody agreed with me that I should have taken Freddie Moore to France – even Pops. But I have very simple things that I do, and that's what I look for in another musician. I looked to Pops and Freddie just to keep the rhythm going, and then I added the garnishing with the barbecue sauce. I don't want a guy fooling around. That's why I used to use guys like Wellman Braud. I thought Oscar Pettiford was a good bass player, too. I used him on that Bill Coleman date back in New York in 1944, with Joe Eldridge, Roy's brother. Pettiford's playing was clear. I like to hear the sound, that it's blending in pretty good.

We traveled to France on the *Hibernian* and we came back on the *Ile de France*. They had jam sessions on the ship, but I didn't play. I'm superstitious about the piano. When I go into a club I never touch the piano until I actually play. People don't understand that. When they want to get a sound check I say, "Well, get it, but get it without me. I don't need a sound check." Everybody has some superstitions. And I've never owned a piano. My mother bought a piano for me once: we moved the same day and I left it right there.

After we returned from France I went up to Music Inn, where Marshall Stearns had these workshops. There were concerts put on by musicians from Rutgers – I think they were called the Rutgers Jazz Ensemble – and they had a whole slew of musicians on hand – Billy Taylor, Milt Jackson, Mahalia Jackson – any person you name, they came up there. I'm sure they must have taped all those things, so that must be some kind of history.

Then I went and joined Henry "Red" Allen at the Metropole. The band played five nights a week. This was a turning point, because I was working with someone who understood me and knew that I kidded a lot but most of the time I meant what I said. I stayed with Red eight years, until he got sick. Red was my best friend and I considered myself his best friend. He was hell to get along with musically because he was so sensitive, but I got along with him by telling him I made him sound good. And it was true. I knew the main ingredients of that particular pie.

When I quit the band, it was out at the Blue Spruce Inn on Long Island. That's where we made the record *Feeling Good*. Now let me tell you about that record. The Saturday night before the record date I said, "Red, I'm getting sick and tired of you again, so I gotta go."

He said, "Bye."

So on Sunday we were off. And Monday he had this recording engagement with John Hammond for *Feeling Good*. And I knew that he would get Lannie Scott to go in as substitute. But I also knew that Lannie didn't know the tunes: he hadn't been playing with Red for eight years. So this Monday night I went out. I got in my car and I said, "Well, I might as well go help this turkey out," meaning Red. So I got in the car and drove all the way out to Long Island. When I walked in, John Hammond and Frank Driggs were there with Red. And Red said to John Hammond, "Here's this politician now."

And I said, "Well, Red. Come on, man, I came out to make you sound good."

So we made *Feeling Good*, *Cherry*, and all those other things. And that was the last time I played with Red, August 1965.

Then a strange thing happened. A few months later he called me and said, "You know what? You're losing one of your best friends." I didn't know what the hell he was talking about. But he had cancer. And I said, "Well, so what?" And this is the way I used to talk to him. "So, I'm losing one of my best friends? If you're talking about yourself, you're not my best friend." Although he was. Shortly after he died, in 1967, I decided I'd had it in music, so then I got out again.

6

Crowned King of Boogie Woogie

In the 1960s I was more interested in political activities and community affairs, though I was still working in music, in and out. There were lots of different movements that had been formed in Harlem. One of the movements, well, it's not a movement really, was first organized many years ago: the NAACP – the National Association for the Advancement of Colored People – they have served a definite need. They are nationwide; they have branches in the various communities throughout America. And then there was another, the Black Nationalist movement – I'm speaking about the movement that came out of Marcus Garvey, the "Back to Africa" movement. These people, many years ago, Sophie and Arthur Reed, and many of the disciples of Marcus Garvey, fought a pretty brave fight on 125th Street so that Negroes could get jobs in many of the stores there. So when you look at the overall picture, all the various movements, I was always reminded when I was out on the street talking to the people in Harlem, I always painted this picture for them: the black man in America has a real problem in that, if he lives in 122nd Street and he has to come to 125th Street, these are some of the things he is confronted with, and it can prove confusing. He has to pass a Catholic church, a church of God in Christ, the Protestant church, he has to pass the NAACP, the Urban League, he has to pass the YMCA, the YWCA, the Black Nationalist movement and the Moslem movement – all of these movements, within two or three blocks, he had to be confronted with. So it kind of made him confused about the way he was going.

There were so may movements because I don't believe we had the true leadership that we needed. We need a messiah, we need someone to come out of the ranks that can really lead us on to the success that we should be able to enjoy in America. We've got to have a man that has a personality of a prince and lovely words and charm and beauty and all these things. He has to win genuine friends from the people. We need to unite the people, make them a part of the integrated picture in America.

I think that an important factor in achieving this is by education. I think that we have to have a different kind of educational programme. So back in the 1960s I was involved in community activities dealing with young people. I was head of a community action group called Neighborhood Board no.2. And I used to take my money and take responsibility for expenses. I did things like putting on a trip. I believe that if young people living in a ghetto can go out of the ghetto and see what's outside, it'll give them some aspiration – some desire. You know, it's an incentive. I remember one trip when I sent ten kids to Washington, to the capital. And then they all wrote essays, and I gave three prizes: $100 for the first, $50 for the second and $25 for the third, plus trip and food. And then I had two adults travel with them. Then I had another thing when they had that fair in Canada; I took 300 kids to the exposition in Montreal. And I'd take 200 kids to the baseball game. Sometimes I'd get given the tickets, but if the guy said, "Well, I can't give you but 100 tickets," well, I'd just buy the other 100 myself.

That was gratifying. You know, I felt good about the whole thing really. I just think we don't pay enough attention to kids. For example, I think that today, to just speak of brash things like sex and all that – discussing the raw things of life – is wrong: sometimes you can introduce innocent kids to raw things that they never thought about doing. It's all right if an adult in a confidential way talks to them. I don't think that boys and girls should be sitting in a room talking about safety methods, how not to get pregnant and all that business. Because there's a lot of young people that don't even know about it, and when you introduce them, then they become curious. That's not really the proper way.

What I really wanted to do more than anything was get the New York school system to introduce in their curriculum black music history, so that when kids go to a music class and hear Aaron Copland they can also hear Duke Ellington and Louis Armstrong. They can hear, like, Larry Adler and Little Walter. Several years ago we got them to invite a black astronaut to come to Harlem, to give the black kids an opportunity to see a black astronaut and to know that a black man can be involved in the space program. I think that's very important. I've always wanted to do something about jazz history, to let the kids have the facts about this great culture.

I've always been interested in trying to stimulate local interest in activities like the Jazz Festival Society in Philadelphia, and I founded the Harlem Jazz Festival Society here in New York with my wife, Nancy. I haven't done anything important with it, but I think that we ought to build this kind of interest in jazz in black communities. We should be creating a sort of incubator for the young people, and out of that can evolve more of the original kind of things that jazz needs. For example, Duke Ellington died several years ago. But what about carrying his music on? What about the heritage, the roots, the tradition? I'm amazed that Mercer Ellington didn't keep the band alive. So where's the incubator, where are the creators coming out of Duke's idiom? Billy Taylor has done one hell of a job for modern jazz. He's been in on all of the committees where the money's allocated and appropriated and where the plans are formulated, and his Jazzmobile has been a great success. He's accomplished things, and I have great respect for him.

Then I had an interest in the law. What I did a lot of times was help guys in trouble by asking the courts to release them into my custody. I'd give a character reference. And I got well known with most of the politicians and attorneys. One time I was in court and the public defender didn't really know who I was. He requested that his client be released into my custody. But the defendant wasn't in court, and the judge said, "Repeat that when the defendant gets here." So when the defendant came in the lawyer said to the judge,

"Your honor, I request that my client be released into the custody of Sam Price." The judge leaned back in his chair, pushed his glasses up onto his head, and said, "I hereby allow the release of the defendant into the custody of Mr Samuel B. Price." That's how well I got to be known.

Another time I got a guy named Pistol Pete out of jail. He was a big guy, six foot six, and he'd had a duel with the police in Times Square. I took him with me when I went out to this record company that owed me money. Pete had his hat brim pulled down and his hand in his pocket. Everybody was looking at us. When we got to the guy's office I opened the door and Pete said, "Is that him, boss?" The guy took one look at Pete and said, "Here's your money." I don't know what the hell Pete was gonna do. We were as clean as two chittlins 'cause Pete was on parole. He wasn't allowed to carry a gun.

Up until a few years ago I was still very active in politics. I worked on behalf of Hubert Humphrey, Lyndon Johnson, Adam Clayton Powell and a lot of those people. I was involved in Harlem. I introduced the idea of jazz music into a political campaign. The late Bill O'Dwyer, who was mayor of New York – only he wasn't mayor then – was sort of slipping in popularity. So what I did was I hired 30 musicians and we went right down Broadway playing *Flying Home*. And Bill O'Dwyer was elected. I don't say that the music made him win, but I know it didn't hurt him. You always have to think of a good idea. And we had people giving out leaflets; I used to organize that kind of thing.

Another thing I did in the 1960s was run a meat company. A friend of mine wanted to set up as competition with a sausage manufacturer. So we organized a company called Down Home Meat Products, and I had a big party and reception for a whole lot of other firms.

In 1969 Louis Jordan was supposed to go to Europe to play, and I understand his people put the pressure on him in Vegas and wouldn't let him leave. This had caused quite a problem: the promoters lost a lot of money, and they wanted somebody else to come that could fulfill the engagements

and appease the impresarios. Somebody told Jean Marie
Monestier about me. I have a good name in Europe. So
Monestier invited me to come to Europe to play and I took
the contract. I engaged a drummer, Candy McDonald. It was
really a whirlwind thing because I met Candy McDonald at
12 o'clock noon. He didn't have a passport and his drums
were put away for "safekeeping" in a pawn shop. We had to
get his drums out of pawn, go to the State Department and
get a passport, pick up the airline tickets and be at the airport
by seven o'clock. We managed all of this, and when we got
to Paris we went on to Bordeaux to meet Monestier and to
start the tour. We played in a lot of cities and enjoyed a big
success.

So I after the tour I went back to Bordeaux and did this
record thing for Monestier's label, Black & Blue – piano solo.
And it was agreed that he was to give me $1000 in advance,
that I was to receive a royalty, and that the rights were mine
– that I would retain the American rights. He gave me $500,
and then another $500, which was $1000, but then it seemed
I was never able to get any reports that were accurate. Some
time after, in 1975, I made some more recordings for him,
including *West End Boogie*, which was a big record. Now he
agreed to give me an advance and I told him he could have
the publisher's rights for five years. That was verbally what
we agreed. I was in the recording studio in Paris and
Monestier came in and gave me the money, and I just
signed. What it said in the contract was "Sammy Price
hereby sells all his rights to all his songs to Black & Blue."
Now I spoke with my lawyer. I didn't mind signing away the
rights for five years to a publisher, but I wrote all those
songs, and I felt I was entitled to my royalties as an artist. So
I wrote a letter and said if they didn't send me my royalties I
would go to the Inland Revenue and the American Consulate and tell them. Eventually I got a check and a letter
saying, "Dear Sammy, I'm not scared of your foolish
pranks."

I did record for Monestier again, though. That was in 1977,
when I went on a tour with Johnny Letman. We had Freddy

Lonzo on trombone, George Kelly on tenor sax, Bill Pemberton on bass and Ronnie Cole on drums. Lonzo, a young man from New Orleans, is a good musician and one of the few promising trombone players that I've heard from Louisiana. He's still young, but he's steeped in the tradition of jazz – sliding, glissing, growling and using mutes and all that. During that tour we played in Yugoslavia, in Portugal, in France – all over. The highlight was when I introduced Johnny Letman and said, "Ladies and gentlemen, I would like to present a young man from America who is following in the footsteps of Louis Armstrong. Louis Armstrong has gone and will not return, so I'm going to ask each of you here in this room to close your eyes and sit back and reminisce as Johnny Letman plays *Sleepy Time Down South*." It was fantastic. In Portugal, in Cascais, he did *Hello Dolly* and *Sleepy Time Down South* and we got a five-minute standing ovation. That happened to me once before, in Barcelona, Spain, in 1956. When these people stood up so long I thought I'd done something wrong. I said, "What the hell did I do wrong?" They said, "You're a big hit."

That's one thing I could never understand, why artists cannot get their right royalties. I don't think that people should be able to use your material like it's in the public domain. After all, we have copyright laws and patent offices so that you can restrain a person from using your material, and I think that every person has a right to some kind of royalty for what he's created or participated in. You know what I think should happen? That if a man is a musician and he's played in terms of years, that he should get something like a musician's honorarium. Say he's been a professional musician for 20 years, he should start receiving some kind of compensation for all the music that's being played in America. They could put it in his social security if he's old enough. That's the fairest way I can think of. Of course some guys, like Jimmy Blanton, would get short-changed, because they died so early. ASCAP, BMI and the union has something like that, but it only seems to go to certain people.

I made a lot of records where I got nothing, absolutely

nothing. It's just hard to get your royalties: you don't know how to find a way. Rather than have a slaughter on Tenth Avenue, you just let it go. You figure that if a guy got nerve enough to just take your material when you're looking right at him, then what can you do?

Jimmy Rushing and I fell out about two tunes I wrote that we recorded for Vanguard in 1954. What happened was we were going to become a team, and Steve Allen wanted us to do a show, wanted us to do *Leave me* and *How you want your lovin' done?* on the show. So we were partners. Well, they only gave me $290 for playing the music, and they gave him $650 for singing it. We were a team, so I said, "Jimmy, it's no more than fair to divide the money." And then we had this big thing at the union: it became a big mess, almost like a Masonic lodge meeting. Cliff Grover said, "Well, Jimmy, if you and Sammy were friends when you had nothing, and when you got something you shared together, then when you get a little more you want it all, well, that's not fair." So that's why I try to stay away from writing any songs for anybody. I do my own thing.

The same sort of thing happened later with Jonah Jones. We'd made this record in 1955 for Jazztone which had a lot of my original tunes. When Jonah became famous the record came out again, but on the jacket it said "Jonah Jones: Trumpets on Tour." That was brazen: "Trumpets on Tour," with Jonah's name on it. And on the back it said "Sam Price and his KayCee Stompers." Now how the hell's he gonna be both of us? So one day I needed some money, and I went right up to Jonah and said, "You're gonna jump out of that window or go to your desk and write me a check. What's it gonna be?"

Another thing that's disturbing to me is that musicians are taken advantage of when they play. For example, take a blues singer today: they give him say $500 a week, which is a good salary for a guy that ain't making no money, and they book him for 21 concerts in Europe. So he plays the concerts, they give him $500 a week, and that's three weeks, $1500. And then he gets right back on the plane and the impresario

is left with all the money; all the musician got was uppercuts
and $500 a week for three weeks. I think that when an artist
goes to Europe he should have to report to a representative
of the American government, like a consulate, and that
might make the impresarios a little more straight with the
guy.

Sometimes impresarios really don't intend to pay more
than the minimum. He'll buy you a suit, give you a bottle of
whiskey, if your rent's due at home he'll pay it, and say,
"Come on, you're going to Europe." And what fool wouldn't
go for that if he's in debt? I know a guy who called me from
London, crying, wanted to know what he could do. He was
in London, but what had happened had happened in
Germany, and the contract was signed in France. So I said,
"Nothin' to do but come on home." By the time he'd gone to
the consulate in France or in Germany he'd have been
starving to death. He had a good solid contract, but no way
to enforce it, so he came on home.

Today you don't have anything like the bandleaders and
the organized groups you used to have. Years ago you had
the Savoy Sultans, Louis Jordan's Tympany Five – you name
it, and you had a group. But today you don't have any of
that. All you have is All Stars, like Sammy Price and his
Friends. So some guy says, "Sammy Price is playing with
some of his friends." And some of them are his enemies.
That's because impresarios match up musicians instead of
letting musicians get guys that they can play with. And
that's what's killed bandleaders.

Always, whenever I've been involved in music, there have
been exciting things happening. In 1975 I went to Pescara in
Italy. We were having a piano summit, and Ray Bryant and
Art Hodes and a whole host of musicians were there. And
when we got into the park where we were to play, this guy
Don Cherry, the free-style jazz musician, got on the stage
and he wouldn't let us play. The kids wanted to come in free,
but I told them, "I came all this distance to play for money,
and if you come here to see me you got to pay, 'cause they

got to pay me." So that particular night the concert was canceled, and the next night they must have had 500 soldiers in that park.

I think it was the same year that Phil Schaap asked me to come over to the West End Cafe to talk with him on radio station KCRC. And I went back to the West End, and I predicted that it would become one of the real musical arenas in America and that people would have an opportunity to enjoy real jazz in a real atmosphere. I was asked at the West End to mention the ten best records that I've made during my career. Number one, I'd place *I'm coming Virginia*, which I made with Red Allen, number two, *Back Home* with Sidney Bechet, and number three *Up Above my Head* with Rosetta Tharpe. After that, *I cover the waterfront* with Doc Cheatham and *Freight Train Blues* with Trixie Smith and Sidney Bechet. Then there was a tune I wrote back in the 1950s called *My Lonesome Heart*, which I recorded with the Blusicians; that was very nice. Then I recorded *Death Letter Blues* with Ida Cox and *Precious Memories* with Rosetta Tharpe and Marie Knight. The next best thing that I thought I liked was Doc Cheatham playing *What can I say dear after I say I'm sorry* – I just can never forget that – and the last was the *Manhattan Blues*, which I made with Jonah Jones. Those are the best ten records as far as I'm concerned.

There are some guys who try to tell you how great a musician is, or how he can't play. What they say about me is that I talk too much. But I talk because that's my prerogative; I can talk if I want to. I came through the period of jazz from the late teens until today, and I like to think I have something to say – that I'm not just talking. I know, for example, that Earl Hines was a great stylist and that he created the jazz piano idiom as we know it. There were lots of stride piano players, but they were not that well known. Guys like Fats Waller, who used to play over a radio station in Cincinnati, really had an opportunity to be creative. But you gotta remember that a lot of these musicians had managers who were in the way, and they prevented a man from really playing how he would like to play and thinking how he would like to think. Yes, money could really change a guy's mind.

And then I liked Charlie Christian. I saw him when he was just a kid playing around in the mud. I think Harry, his brother, probably started him off, encouraged him. You see, you can't teach a person to play an instrument; he's got to have a good ear and be inspired by something. It's like if you're on the avenue and there's a crowd of people and they keep brushing up against you, you'll get whatever they've got on them on you. And then, if you're attentive and conscious and have any kind of ability, it can be developed. I didn't see Charlie again until I saw him in New York, after John Hammond brought him. He was with Benny Goodman then, and very rarely played otherwise.

Benny was one of the big white bandleaders who used black musicians. He knew what was good for him. He used them in a sensible way and he paid attention. Plus I think he had an innate ability to know what black musicians were playing; he was like a third cousin. He played what would fit in with what they were playing.

I really don't know what to say as far as whether I've made a contribution musically. That, history will have to determine, and usually they don't decide whether you've done anything until after you're dead and gone. But I've made over 100 boogie-woogie records: I've made boogie-woogie in every country, from the *Denmark Boogie* to the *Munchen Boogie*. I just do it as a lark, because when I do it it's funny on stage and the people like the music.

One of the things I did in New York in the 1970s was I opened the Crawdaddy Restaurant at the Roosevelt Hotel – that was a New Orleans restaurant – and then I worked at the Cookery down in the Village for Barney Josephson, the man who owned Cafe Society. Alberta Hunter was there, but I never accompanied her. We was just good friends: she called me "a fat tub of lard" and I called her "that old lady" – those were our greetings to each other. We went back to the Chicago days in the 1930s, when we used to live in the

Southway Hotel. I used to stop in at the Cookery every now and then to see her. When I was there I was with a trio – piano, guitar and bass. They didn't allow any horns because of the licensing. One of the guys with me was a guitar player named Copeland.

I'll tell you about when I was at the Crawdaddy Club. That was formerly the room where Guy Lombardo played. They had a big birthday party for me there, a big celebration, and Eubie Blake crowned me King of Boogie-Woogie. As he put the crown on my head he said, "Sammy, I crown you King of Boogie-Woogie. But I don't kiss men." That was quite an experience for me.

I've made a lot of records in Europe. I recorded for Polydor, Vogue and Black & Blue in France, and for Black Lion in London. I made a lot of records which helped me become well known abroad. I've worked all over Europe, too. There's not much difference between the audiences in Europe and the audiences in the United States. You wouldn't believe it, but I talk when I play – I talk to the audience. And do you know that most of the time they understand me even if I speak in English. If I say something funny, they laugh. For example, I was in London and the agent had me going to Bridgend – that's in Wales. So I was on the stage, talking, and the impresario asked, "Well, how do you like Wales?"

I said, "Wales, what do you mean, Wales? I thought Wales was in Scotland." And everybody fell about laughing. And the next thing I knew I was in a town called Slough. But I called it "Slew." I always intentionally mispronounced it, and whenever I'd say it they'd all crack up.

When I was in England that time I was working with British musicians. I worked in London at the Pizza on the Park and Pizza Express on Dean Street. It was nice. The worst thing that happened to me on that tour was when I was going up north, and I was at St Pancras Station. I used to overburden myself with bags, and I had six bags, my typewriter and my umbrella. And I got everything onto the train but the typewriter. I left it sitting on the platform. And the train started off and I had to run and get my typewriter and run and get back on the train. I always travel with so much luggage: you never know what you might need.

In 1982 I went to Australia and played with Geoff Bull in Sydney, Canberra - all around. I'd always wanted to go to Australia, and the tour was very successful. Just after I returned, in October, I had a call from Mr William Heck, the general manager of the Copley Plaza Hotel in Boston. Mr Heck offered me a job as a solo pianist at the hotel, but instead I made a proposal that I have a jazz trio with Willis "Gator" Jackson on tenor sax and Carl Goodwin on drums. After a discussion it was agreed that we would try out my idea, and after two weeks business was so good that Mr Heck and myself became good friends. I wasn't sure that the people in Boston would go for my kind of jazz, but from the start they went for my talking to them, as well as shaking hands and remembering names and talking about their kids. So I had a successful two-month on, two-month off engagement.

The following year, just three days before one of my opening dates at the Copley Plaza, Willis Jackson had to go into the hospital. This was a bit of a cliffhanger for me, as it took some doing to get a replacement for Willis. So then I had Andy McGhee, who I first met in Paris in 1957, and the trio worked out real good.

I met Dan Kochakian, who had collected my records and wanted me to make a recording for his label, Whiskey, Women & . . .. I was worried about doing the date, having come from a church family, as I didn't think people would go for a name like that. But you know money in the hand can change a person's mind, so I made the record, titled *Play it Again, Sam*, and we sold quite a few albums, because he also had a very nice jazz magazine published each month, and it was so popular. Dan Kochakian also made a deal with a company and had some of my earlier records reissued.

I was trying to keep busy all this time because I hadn't really gotten over my wife's death, which was in December 1978. I went out of my way to work with the newspapers, the

TV and the radio. Ron Delecasse was a radio announcer who became one of my good friends and always had me on his show when I returned to Boston. It was a good feeling for me to have this exposure, to have people lined up waiting for me to sign their records. The *Globe* and other papers were talking about Sammy Price and his music drawing large crowds to the Copley Plaza Hotel.

What I had in mind was to visit some of the colleges in Boston and have a chance to talk about the black jazz being played. The first thing I did was to compose a boogie-woogie, and then I asked Mr Heck to invite the head of Harvard Music School to come to the hotel so that I could present the school with my piece and also create a Sammy Price Scholarship. I was happy that the idea took hold. I went to Harvard one night to hear Illinois Jacquet, who was artist-in-residence there, as he was giving a concert. Halfway through the concert Jacquet invited me to play a number with the band. I didn't want to play, but the audience insisted, and that was when I realized how much publicity I had received in Boston. I played the *Harvard Boogie* and I broke up the concert.

Several days later I received a letter wanting to know if I would consent to be the artist-in-residence at Harvard for 1985. While I was still making up my mind I received a Certificate of Fellowship from Dr Bok, the President of Harvard, which really knocked me off my feet. I had a flashback to all the concerts I had played for the Jeunesses Musicales in France in 1956. The big difference was that I would have a chance to talk to the youth and try to set some of the records straight. It was decided that the starting date would be Thursday October 17th, and I was to have special guests.

So what happened was that I ran a series of classes for musicians and listeners called "The History of the Blues and Early Jazz." And I gave lecture demonstrations of blues styles on the piano. Rare jazz films by Jack Bradley the film collector were shown to help to get everyone ready for the concert to be held at the theater. I made a request that extra pianos be on hand so that the students could play, as I was determined that the program would give the students a free hand. At the end of the program we had a concert, like a school graduation, with the young people in their best dress to show what they had learned. That night the house was packed and people were saying that it had been a great success.

It was hard for me to realize that I had been playing for 60 years, from the time the music teacher had told my mother that I would never play music and to forget it. I also remembered what Booker T. Washington's daughter had said to me several years later – that I had a feel for music and that my natural ability would carry me far up the ladder. I felt good about the whole thing, as I had promised my daughter Sharon and Janice Davis, a family friend, that I would press hard to make the program work well.

The workshops at Harvard opened the door for me to appear at other schools, and the following year I played at Roxbury Community College, Smith College and Wilkes College.

For my 62 years as a musician I have to thank so many people around the world, which would include Jack Kapp, Dave Kapp, Mayo Williams of Decca Records, Barney Josephson of the Cafe Society Downtown, Billy Rose for picking me to play in the Broadway play *Clash by Night*, Joe Glaser, Milt Gabler, A. P. Joseph, Kathie Kasch, Daniel and his wife Ellen, my surrogate children who are dear to me, Mr and Mrs William Heck, Mr and Mrs Allen Trumaine of the Copley Plaza Hotel, Boston, who made my life beautiful during my four years in Boston, and Hans Zurburg of the jazz festival in Berne, Switzerland, for always remembering me at festival time. I would like to sum up my career with these words: I told Eubie Blake that I would like to live to be 100, but I don't think I can take it.

Discography

compiled by Bob Weir

This discography includes all traced recordings on which Sammy Price has played. Original issues only are given. These are 78 r.p.m. 10" records unless presented in italics, in which case they are 12" LPs; other formats, e.g., EPs, CDs, are individually indicated. Vocalists are indicated by initials following a song title, except where the record credit is to the vocalist, in which case he or she sings on every item from the session.

A selective list of 12" LPs, containing the most recent or the most complete issues of Sammy Price's recordings, is appended.

The following collectors provided helpful information and advice: Alan Balfour, Peter Carr, Derek Coller, John Curtis, David Griffiths, John Holley, Dan Kochakian, Bob Laughton, Bill Rankin, Howard Rye, Len Salmon, Bernard Shirley, Roy Simonds and Eric Townley.

Abbreviations

alt	alternative take
an	announcer
arr	arranger
as	alto saxophone
bj	banjo
bs	baritone saxophone
c	cornet
cl	clarinet
d	drums
db	double bass
elb	electric bass

flh	flugelhorn
g	guitar
hca	harmonica
mst	master take
o	organ
p	piano
ss	soprano saxophone
t	trumpet
tb	trombone
ts	tenor saxophone
v	vocal
vib	vibraphone
vn	violin
wb	washboard

Countries of origin

All records listed are of United States origin, unless otherwise indicated:

Aa	Austria	E	England	I	Italy
Au	Australia	F	France	Sw	Sweden
C	Canada	G	West Germany	Sz	Switzerland
D	Denmark	H	Holland		

1929
October 26   Dallas

Sam Price and his Four Quarters

'Kid Lips' (t); Bert Johnson (tb); Sammy Price (p); Percy Darensbourg (bj)

DAL464   Blue rhythm stomp   Brunswick 7136

Bert Johnson (tb), with Sammy Price (p); Effie Scott (comments)

DAL465   Nasty but nice   Brunswick 7136

Effie Scott (v), with Bert Johnson (tb) −1; Sammy Price (p); Percy Darensbourg (g)

DAL468	Lonesome hut blues −1	Vocalion 1461
DAL469	Sunshine special	Vocalion 1461

NB Price not on DAL466 The right string but the wrong yo yo/DAL 467 Sweet sweet mama (Brunswick 7123), by Douglas Finnell and his Royal Stompers, from this session.

1938
May 8   New York

Cow Cow Davenport (v), with Joe Bishop (flh); Sammy Price (p); Teddy Bunn (g, v); Richard Fullbright (db)

63763-A	Don't you loud-mouth me	Decca 7486
63764-A	I ain't no iceman	Decca 7462
63765-A	The mess is here	Decca 7813
63766-A	Railroad blues	Decca 7462
63767-A	That'll get it (plus TB,v)	Decca 7486

1938
May 12   New York

Jimmie Gordon (v) and his Vip Vop Band

Joe Bishop (flh); Sammy Price (p); Teddy Bunn (g); Richard Fullbright (db)

63756-A	Crying my blues away	Decca 7519
63757-A	Fast life	Decca 7474
63758-A	Sail with me	Decca 7519
63759-A	Lonesome bedroom blues	Decca 7490
63760-A	Alberta Alberta	Decca 7490
63761-A	She's doin' it now	Decca 7474
63762-A	Keep your nose out of other people's business	Decca 7624

1938
May 25   New York

Ebony Three (v trio), with Buster Bailey (cl); Sammy Price (p); Richard Fullbright (db); O'Neill Spencer (d)

63862-A	Swing low, sweet chariot	Decca 7527
63863-A	Go down Moses	Decca 7527
63864-A	Heartbroken blues	Decca 7503
63865-	Mississippi moan	Decca 7503

1938
May 26   New York

Trixie Smith (v), with Charlie Shavers (t); Sidney Bechet (cl); Sammy Price (p); Teddy Bunn (g); Richard Fullbright (db); O'Neill Spencer (d)

63866-A	Freight train blues	Decca 7489
63867-A	Trixie blues	Decca 7469
63868-A	My daddy rocks me	Decca 7469
63869-A	My daddy rocks me, no.2	Decca 7617
63870-A	He may be your man (but he comes to me sometime)	Decca 7528
63871-A	Jack I'm mellow	Decca 7528
63872-A	Lady be good (instrumental)	Unissued-rejected
63877-A	My unusual man	Decca 7489

Grant and Wilson
(Coot Grant and Kid Wesley Wilson, v duet); Coot Grant (v)−1 Same personnel except Wellman Braud (db) replaces Richard Fullbright

63873-A	Uncle Joe	Decca 7500
63874-A	I am a woman	*Time-Life STLJ50098*
63875-A	Toot it, Brother Armstrong −1	Decca 7500
63876-A	Blue monday on Sugar Hill	Decca 7500

NB The standard issue of Decca 7500 contains Uncle Joe/Blue monday on Sugar Hill, but a few copies have Toot it Brother Armstrong/Blue monday on Sugar Hill.

1938
August 11   New York

Blue Lu Barker (v) with Danny Barker's Fly Cats
Henry Red Allen (t); Buster Bailey (cl); Sammy Price (p); Danny Barker (g); Wellman Braud (db); O'Neill Spencer (d)

64432-A	You're going to leave the old home, Jim	Decca 7560
64433-A	New Orleans blues	Decca 7538
64434-A	He caught that B & O	Decca 7506
64435-A	Don't you make me high	Decca 7506

1938
September 13   New York

Bea Foote (v), with Charlie Shavers (t); J.C. Higginbotham (tb); Buster Bailey (cl); Sammy Price (p); unknown (g, db, d)

64658-A	Try and get it	Decca 7535
64659-A	Jive lover	Decca 7535
64660-A	If it don't fit, don't force it	Unissued-rejected
64661-A	I want a long time daddy	Decca 7554

1938
November 22   New York

Blue Lu Barker (v) with Danny Barker's Fly Cats
Benny Carter (t); Buster Bailey (cl); Sammy Price (p); Danny Barker (g); Wellman Braud (db); O'Neill Spencer (d)

64767-A	I feel like lying in another woman's husband's arms	Unissued-rejected
64768-A	Give me some money	Unissued-rejected
64769-	I got ways like the devil	Decca 7560
64770-A	That made him mad	Decca 7538

1939
March 6   New York

Johnnie Temple (v), with Sammy Price (p); Teddy Bunn (g); unknown (db)

65203-A	Jelly roll Bert	Decca 7573
65204-A	Up today and down tomorrow	Decca 7632
65205-	Getting old blues	Decca 7599
65206-A	The sun goes down in blood	Decca 7632

65207-A	Better not let my good gal catch you here (My regular woman)	Decca 7583
65208-	If I could holler	Decca 7599

1939
March 24   New York

Lee Brown (v) with Sam Price's Fly Cats
Charlie Shavers (t); Buster Bailey (cl); Sammy Price (p); probably Teddy Bunn (g); O'Neill Spencer (d)

65266-A	Moanin' dove (omit Shavers & Bailey)	Decca 7575
65269-A	New little girl, little girl	Decca 7575
65270-A	I can lay it on down	Decca 7626
65271-A	Down by the M & O (omit Shavers & Bailey)	Decca 7587
65272-A	Jeff Davis highway (omit Shavers & Bailey)	Decca 7587
65273-A	Let me be your bo weavil (omit Shavers & Bailey)	Decca 7790

Lether McGraw (v) with Sam Price's Fly Cats
Same personnel minus (g)

65267-A	Do your duty	Decca 7580
65268-A	Low down dirty groundhog	Decca 7580

1939
March 30   New York

Peetie Wheatstraw (William Bunch) (v), with Sammy Price (p); Teddy Bunn (g); O'Neill Spencer (d)

65310-A	Possum den blues (omit Bunn)	Decca 7589
65310-B	Possum den blues	Decca 7589
65311-A	Little low mellow mama	Decca 7578
65312-A	A working man's blues	Decca 7641
65313-A	One to twelve (Just as show)	Decca 7605
65314-A	Let's talk things over	Decca 7605
65315-A	Sinking sun blues	Decca 7578
65316-A	Easy way blues	Decca 7641
65317-A	Machine gun blues	Decca 7778

1939
April 18   New York

Ollie Shepard (v) and his Kentucky Boys
Chu Berry (ts); Sammy Price (p); unknown (d)

65420-A	New low down dirty shame	Decca 7585
65421-A	The numbers blues	Decca 7585
65422-A	Sweetest thing born	Decca 7629
65423-A	Shepard blues (Pig latin blues)	Decca 7602
65424-A	Outdoor blues (add Lonnie Johnson, g)	Decca 7613
65425-A	Sugar woman blues	Decca 7602
65426-A	Hell is so low down	Decca 7716
65427-A	My dripping blood blues	Decca 7613
65428-A	Blues 'bout my gal	Decca 7639

1939
April 20   New York

Blue Lu Barker (v) with Danny Barker's Fly Cats
Charlie Shavers (t); Chu Berry (ts); Sammy Price (p); Danny Barker (g); unknown (db, d)

65433-A	Scat skunk	Decca 7813
65434-A	Nix on those lush heads	Decca 7588
65435-A	Buy me some juice	Unissued-rejected
65436-A	Georgia grind	Decca 7588

1939
April 27   New York

Harlem Stompers (v group) including Hester Lancaster (v), with Sammy Price (p); unknown (t, g, db, d)

65486-A	The monkey swing	Decca 7600
65487-A	Jammin' in Georgia	Decca 7616
65488-A	My understanding man	Decca7600
65489-A	Serenade to a jitterbug	Decca 7616

1939
April 28   New York

Jimmie Gordon (v) with his Vip Vop Band

Frankie Newton (t); Pete Brown (as); Sammy Price (p); Zutty Singleton (d)

65494-A	Get your mind out of the gutter	Decca 7611
65495-A	Delhia	Decca 7592
65496-A	Do that thing	Decca 7611
65497-A	The mojo blues	Decca 7702
65498-A	St Peter blues	Decca 7592
65499-A	If walls could talk	Decca 7624

Selah Jubilee Singers (v gospel sextet), with Sammy Price (p)

65500-A	Royal telephone	Decca 7607
65501-A	Traveling shoes	Decca 7628
65502-A	How happy I am	Decca 7628
65503-A	What he done for me	Decca 7598
65504-A	I want Jesus to walk around my bedside	Decca 7607
65505-A	Take my hand precious Lord (Lead me on)	Decca 7598

1939
May 18   New York

Georgia White (v), with Sammy Price (p); Teddy Bunn (g); John Lindsay (db)

65597-A	The way I'm feelin'	Decca 7596
65598-A	Married woman blues	Decca 7596
65599-A	How do you think I feel	Decca 7652
65600-A	Fire in the mountain	Decca 7608
65601-A	When the sun turns to gray (I'll be back)	Decca 7608

1939
May 26   New York

Fat Hayden (v), with Sammy Price (p); Teddy Bunn (g); unknown (db)

65657-A	A brownskin gal (is the best gal after all)	Decca 7614
65658-A	Voo doo blues	Decca 7614

1939
September 13   Chicago

Johnnie Temple (v), with John Robinson (cl); Sammy Price (p);
Lonnie Johnson (g); John Lindsay (db)

91757-A	Streamline blues	Decca 7660
91758-A	Good Suzie (Rusty knees)	Decca 7643
91759-A	Down in Mississippi	Decca 7643
91760-A	Evil bad woman	Decca 7660
91761-A	Cherry ball	Decca 7678
91762-A	Let's get together	Decca 7678

1939
September 29   Chicago

Jimmie Gordon (v) and his Vip Vop Band

Probably Buster Bennett (as); Sammy Price (p); possibly Ike Perkins
(g); Sid Catlett (d)

91820-A	Nobody knows the trouble I see	Decca 7764
91821-A	The boogie man (plus band, v)	Decca 7661
91822-A	Ease it to me	Decca 7661
91823-A	Henpecked man	Decca 7702

Gene Gilmore (v), with Sammy Price (p); possibly Ike Perkins (g);
Sid Catlett (d)

91824-A	Brown skin woman	Decca 7671
91825-A	Charity blues	Decca 7671

James Carter (v), with Sammy Price (p); possibly Ike Perkins (g);
Sid Catlett (d)

91826-A	Death letter blues	Decca 7681
91827-A	Death cell blues	Decca 7681

1939
November 17   New York

Blue Lu Barker (v) with Danny Barker and his Fly Cats

Henry "Red" Allen (t); Sammy Price (p); Danny Barker (g);
Wellman Braud (db); unknown (d)

66893-A	Deep blue sea blues	Decca 7709
66894-A	Never brag about your man	Decca 7683
66895-A	He's so good	Decca 7695
66896-A	I don't dig you, Jack	Decca 7770

1939
December 13   New York

Blue Lu Barker (v) with Danny Barker and his Fly Cats

Henry "Red" Allen (t); Sammy Price (p); Danny Barker (g);
Wellman Braud (db); probably Sid Catlett (d)

66956-A	Handy Andy	Decca 7709
66957-A	Jitterbug blues	Decca 7713
66958-A	You been holding out too long	Decca 7695
66959-A	Lu's blues	Decca 7770

1940
March 13   New York

Sam Price and his Texas Blusicians

Joe Brown (t); Ed Mullens (t); Don Stovall (as); Ray Hill (ts);
Sammy Price (p, v); Duke Jones (db); Wilbert Kirk (d)

67304-A	Fetch it to me	Decca 7781
67305-A	Cow Cow blues (SP, comments)	Decca 7732
67306-A	Sweepin' the blues away	Decca 7781
67307-A	Swing out in the groove (SP, v)	Decca 7732

1940
April 4   New York

Johnnie Temple (v), with Buster Bailey (cl); Sammy Price (p); Al
Casey (g); Herbert Cowans (d)

67489-A	Good woman blues	Decca 7735
67490-A	Skin and bones woman	Decca 7750
67491-A	I'm cuttin' out	Decca 7772

67492-A	Fireman blues	Decca 7782
67493-A	Lovin' woman blues	Decca 7772
67494-A	Roomin' house blues	Decca 7782
67495-A	Sugar bowl blues	Decca 7735
67496-A	Stick up woman (Let me make this trip with you)	Decca 7750

1940
June 4　Chicago

Jimmie Gordon (v) and his Vip Vop Band
Possibly Buster Bennett (as); Sammy Price (p); unknown (g, db)

93010-A	Trigger Slim blues	Decca 7764
93012-A	(Roll 'em Dorothy) Let 'em jump for joy	Decca 7794
93012-B	L & N blues	Decca 7794

1940
September 26　New York

Sam Price and his Texas Blusicians
Joe Brown (t); Ed Mullens (t); Don Stovall (as); Ray Hill (ts); Sammy Price (p, v); Duke Jones (db); Wilbert Kirk (d)

68149-A	How 'bout that mess	Decca 8505
68150-A	Oh Red (SP, v)	Decca 8505
68151-A	Oh lawdy mama (SP, v)	Decca 7811
68152-A	The dirty dozens (SP, v)	Decca 7811

1940
December 6　New York

Sam Price and his Texas Blusicians
Lem Johnson (cl, ts); Sammy Price (p, v); Duke Jones (db); unknown (d)

| 68457-A | Thinking (SP, v) | Decca 8515 |
| 68459-A | Jumpin' the boogie | Decca 8515 |

Lem Johnson and his Washboard Band
Lem Johnson (cl, v); Sammy Price (p, v); Duke Jones (db); unknown (wb)

68458-A	Queen Street blues (SP, v)	Decca 7820
68460-A	Louise Louise (LJ, v)	Decca 7820

1941
April 3   New York

Sam Price and his Texas Blusicians

Shad Collins (t); Bill Johnson (t); Don Stovall (as); Lester Young (ts); Sammy Price (p); Duke Jones (db); Harold West (d); Sam Theard ("Spo-De-O-Doe Sam") (v)

68920-A	The goon drag (Gone wid de goon)	Decca 8547
68922-A	Lead me daddy straight to the bar (ST, v)	Decca 8649
68923-A	Just jivin' around	Decca 8557

Yack Taylor (v) with Sam Price and his Texas Blusicians
Same personnel, without Sam Theard

68921-A	Things 'bout coming my way	Decca 8557

1941
April 8   New York

Yack Taylor (v), with Sammy Price (p); unknown (g, d)

68951-A	My mellow man	Decca 7836
68952-A	Knockin' myself out	Decca 7836
68953-A	You're gonna go your way and I'm gonna go mine	Decca 7850

Sam Price and his Texas Blusicians
Sammy Price (p, v); unknown (g, d)

68954-A	I lost love (When I lost you)	Decca 8547

1941
June 13   New York

Sam Price and his Texas Blusicians

Chester Boone (t); Floyd Brady (tb); Don Stovall (as); Skippy Williams (ts); Sammy Price (p, v); Ernest Hill (db); Herbert Cowans (d)

69365-A	Do you dig my jive (SP & band, v)	Decca 8575
69366-A	I know how to do it (SP & band, v)	Decca 8566
69367-A	Valetta (SP, v)	Decca 8566
69368-A	Boogie woogie moan	Decca 8575

1941
July 17   New York

(Big) Joe Turner (v), with Sammy Price (p); Leonard Ware (g); Billy Taylor (db)

69523-A	Nobody in mind	Decca 7868
69524-A	Somebody's got to go	Decca 7856
69525-A	Ice man	Decca 7856
69526-A	Chewed up grass (plus band, v)	Decca 7868

1941
July 23   New York

Mabel Robinson (v) with the Four Blackamoors (v group)

Sammy Price (p); unknown (vn, g, db)

69549-A	You don't know my mind	Decca 8580
69550-A	Somebody's getting my love	Decca 8580
69551-A	Don't give up the old love	Decca 8568
69552-A	Search your heart and see	Decca 8568

Yack Taylor (v), with Sammy Price (p); possibly Leonard Ware (g); unknown (d)

69553-A	Don't stop now	Decca 7864
69554-A	Chicago bound blues	Decca 7855
69555-A	Whip it to a jelly	Decca 7855
69556-A	My nightmare jockey	Decca 7864

1941
September 11   New York

Nora Lee King (v), with Sammy Price (p); Ham Jackson (g); probably William "Smitty" Smith (db)

69740-A	Love me	Unissued-rejected

69741-A	Let me rock you home	Decca 7883
68742-A	Yump da da da	Unissued-rejected
69743-	Why don't you do right?	Decca 7866

1941
October 8   New York

Sweet Georgia Brown (v), with Sammy Price (p); Ham Jackson (g); unknown (db)

69789-A	The low down lonely blues	Decca 7880
69790-A	Rock me in the groove	Decca 7871
69791-A	Black cat bone	Decca 7880
69792-A	These low down men blues	Decca 7871

Nora Lee King (v), with Sammy Price (p); Ham Jackson (g); unknown (db)

| 69793-B | Love me | Decca 7870 |
| 69794-A | Yump da da da | Decca 7870 |

1941
October 15   New York

Jimmy Smith and his Sepians

Kenneth Roane (t, ocarina—1); Jimmy Smith (cl, ts); Sammy Price (p); Ham Jackson (g); William "Smitty" Smith (db); unknown (d); Nora Lee King (v)

69817-A	Boy, it's solid groovy (NLK, v)−1	Decca 8618
69818-A	I ain't got nobody to love (NLK, v)	Decca 8591
69819-A	Sporty Joe (NLK, v)−1	Decca 8618
69820-A	Big chump blues (NLK, v)−1	Decca 8591

Ruby Smith (v), with Sammy Price (p); Ham Jackson (g); William "Smitty" Smith (db)

69821-A	Make love to me	Decca 7875
69822-A	Fruit cakin' mama	Decca 7869
69823-A	Black gal	Decca 7869
69824-A	Thinking blues	Decca 7875

1941
December 10   New York

Ruby Smith (v) with Sam Price and his Texas Blusicians
Emmett Berry (t); Ray Hogan (tb); Fess Williams (cl, as); Don Stovall (as); Sammy Price (p); Billy Taylor (db); J.C. Heard (d)

70029-A	Why don't you love me anymore	Decca 8609
70030-A	Harlem gin blues	Decca 8609

Jack Meredith (v) with Sam Price and his Texas Blusicians
Same personnel

70031-A-B	My name is Jim	Unissued-rejected
70032-B	Matchbox blues	Decca 8624

1942
January 20   New York

Mabel Robinson (v) with Sam Price and his Texas Blusicians
Herman Autrey (t); David Young (ts); Sammy Price (p); William Lewis (g); Vernon King (db); O'Neill Spencer (d)

70187-A	Me and my chauffeur	Decca 8601
70188-A	I've got too many blues	Decca 8601

Sam Price and his Texas Blusicians
Same personnel

70189-A	It's all right Jack	Decca 8649
70190-A	Blow, Katy, blow	Decca 8624

1942
February 9   New York

Helen Humes (v) with Pete Brown and his Band
Dizzy Gillespie (t); Jimmy Hamilton (cl); Pete Brown (as); Sammy Price (p); Charlie Drayton (db); Ray Nathan (d)

70299-A	Mound bayou	Decca 8613
70300-A	Unlucky woman (Unlucky blues)	Decca 8613
70301-A	Gonna buy me a telephone	Decca 8625

Nora Lee King (v) with Pete Brown and his Band
Same personnel

70302-A	Cannonball	Decca 8625

1942
March 19   New York

Bea Booze (Muriel Nicholls) (v, g), with Sammy Price (p);
unknown (db, d)

70543-A	If I'm a fool (I'm a fool about the man I love) (omit g)	Decca 8619
70544-A	I love to Georgia Brown so slow	Decca 8629
70545-A	Uncle Sam come and get him	Decca 8619
70546-A	If I didn't love you	Decca 8629

1942
March 26   New York

Bea Booze (Muriel Nicholls) (v, g), with Sammy Price (p);
unknown (db, d)

70570-B	See see rider blues	Decca 8633
70571-	Let's be friends	Decca 8621

1942
March 27   New York

Bea Booze (Muriel Nicholls) (v, g–1), with Sammy Price (p);
unknown (db, d)

70580-B	Catchin' as catch can	Decca 8633
70581-A	War rationin' papa −1	Decca 8621

Nora Lee King (v), with Sammy Price (p); unknown (t, g, db)

70589-A	Deep sea diver	Decca 7891

1942
May 19   New York

Lem Johnson (v), with Sammy Price (p); George Van Eps (g); Haig
Stephens (db)

70760-A	Going down slow	Decca 7895
70761-A	Candy blues	Decca 7895

1942
July 25   New York

Sam Price and his Texas Blusicians

Freddie Webster (t); Don Stovall (as); Sammy Price (p);
unknown (ts, db, d)

71195-A	Teed-up	Decca 8642
71196-A	Frantic	Decca 8642

1944
March 1   New York

Sam Price and his Blusicians/and his Rockin' Rhythm

Bill Coleman (t); Joe Eldridge (as); Ike Quebec (ts); Sammy Price
(p); Oscar Pettiford (db); Harold West (d)

N 1800-1	That's kicks	*Circle CLP-73*
N 1800-2	That's kicks	*Circle CLP-73*
N 1800-3	That's kicks (incomplete)	*Circle CLP-73*
N 1800-4	That's kicks	*Black Jack LP 3012*
N 1801-1	Pluckin' that thing (incomplete)	*Circle CLP-73*
N 1801-2	Pluckin' that thing	Decca 48097
N 1801-3	Pluckin' that thing	*Circle CLP-73*
N 1802-1	Boogie woogie notion (10" LP)	*Brunswick BL58045*
N 1803-1	House rent boogie (false start – p only)	*Circle CLP-73*
N 1803-2	House rent boogie	*Black Jack LP3012*
N 1804-1	Big Joe (incomplete)	*Circle CLP-73*
N 1804-2	Big Joe (false start)	*Circle CLP-73*
N 1804-3	Big Joe	*Circle CLP-73*
N 1804-4	Big Joe	Decca 48097
N1805-1	Boogin' a plenty (false start – as, p, db & d only)	*Circle CLP-73*
N 1805-2	Boogin' a plenty	*Brunswick BL58045*
N 1806-1	Sweet Lorraine	*Black Jack LP3012*
N 1807-1	Honeysuckle rose (false start – p, db & d only)	*Circle CLP-73*
N 1807-2	Honeysuckle rose (incomplete)	*Circle CLP-73*
N 1807-3	Honeysuckle rose (false start – as, p, db & d only)	*Circle CLP-73*
N 1807-4	Honeysuckle rose	*Brunswick BL58045*

1944
March 9   New York

Bea Booze (Muriel Nicholls) (v, g), with Sammy Price (p); Abe Bolar (db); Harold West (d)

71844	Mr Freddie blues	Decca 48033
71845	Uncle Sam took a darn good man	Unissued
71846	Gulf Coast blues	Decca 48033
71847	These young men blues	Decca 8658
71850	Achin' hearted blues	Unissued
71851	So good (plus band, v)	Decca 8658

Perline Ellison (v), with Sammy Price (p); Abe Bolar (db); Harold West (d)

| 71848-A | Razor totin' mama | Decca 7910 |
| 71849-A | New that ain't right | Decca 7910 |

1944
April 6   New York

Christine Chatman (v) and her Orchestra

Mabel Smith (v); Reginald Adams (t); Ralph Bowden (ts); Bill Moore (ts); Sammy Price (p); Roger Jones (db); Horace Washington (d)

71948	Naptown boogie	Decca 8660
71949	Bootin' the boogie (CC & band, v)	Decca 48035
71950	The boogie woogie girl (CC, v)	Decca 48035
71951	Hurry hurry (MS, v)	Decca 8660

NB Mabel Smith was later known as "Big Mabelle".

mid-1944   New York

Sammy Price

Tommy Allinson (t); Dave Nelson (t); Joe Eldridge (as); Paul Bascomb (ts); Sammy Price (p); Jimmy Butts (db); Harold West (d); Bettye Logan (v)

| 72165 | That's the lick | Decca-unissued |
| 72166 | Jumpin' for you | Decca-unissued |

72167	Too late now	Decca-unissued
72168	Jodie man	Decca-unissued

1944
September 26   New York

Sister Rosetta Tharpe (v, g) with the Sam Price Trio
Sammy Price (p); Abe Bolar (db); Harold West (d)

72396-A	Singing in my soul	Decca 8672
72397-A	I claim Jesus first	Decca 8672
72398-A	Strange things happening every day (plus band, v)	Decca 8669
72399-A	Two little fishes and five loaves of bread	Decca 8669

1944
November 13   New York

Warren Evans (v) and his Orchestra
Dick Vance (t); Dave Nelson (t); Benny Morton (tb); George James (as); Joe Eldridge (as); Lem Johnson (ts); Sammy Price (p); Everett Barksdale (g); Billy Taylor (db); Harold West (d)

NSC17	Valetta	National 9007
NSC18	I'm lost	National 9004
NSC19	You've gotta lotta wolf in your heart	National 9007
NSC20	I wonder (Evans & rhythm section only)	National 9003

1944
December 11   New York

Tommy Edwards (v) with Sam Price and his Orchestra
Sammy Price (p); others unknown

72615	Beer bucket love	Decca-unissued
72616	When the deal goes down	Decca-unissued

Warren Evans (v) with probably Sammy Price (p); others unknown

72617	Don't be late	Decca-unissued
72618	Just call on me	Decca-unissued

1945
March 9   New York

Warren Evans (v) with Sam Price and his Orchestra

Freddie Webster (t); George James (as); Sammy Price (p); John Brown (db); Harold West (d)

72763-A	Don't be late	Decca 48015
72764	In the wee small hours of the morning	Decca 48020
72765	Just call on me	Decca 48020
72766-A	Mad about you	Decca 48015

1945
March 27   New York

Sammy Price (as "Jimmy Blythe Jr") (p)

KJ1-1	In a Mezz	Jazz Selection (F) 874
KJ2-1	Those mellow blues	Jazz Selection (F) 874
KJ3-1	Gully low blues	*Storyville (D) SLP137*
KJ4-1	Cow Cow blues	Jazz Selection (F) 878
KJ5-1	133rd Street boogie	*Jazz Selection (F) LP 50045*
KJ6-1	I finally gotcha	King Jazz 145
KJ7-1	Boogin' with Mezz	King Jazz 145
KJ8-1	Callin' 'em home	Jazz Selection (F) 878
KJ9-1	Shakin' loose (Step down, step up)	Jazz Selection (F) 879
KJ9-2	Shakin' loose	Jazz Selection (F) 879
KJ9-3	Shakin' loose	*Storyville (D) SLP821*

Pleasant Joe (Joe Pleasants) (v), with Sammy Price (p)

KJ10	Broken man blues	*Storyville (D) SLP153*
KJ11	New jailhouse blues	*Festival (F) FLD 363*

NB The Jazz Selection 78s were incorrectly titled.

1945
April 14   New York

Albinia Jones (v) with Don Byas' Swing Seven

Dizzy Gillespie (t); Gene Sedric (cl); Don Byas (ts); Sammy Price (p); Leonard Ware (g); Oscar Smith (db); Harold West (d)

NSC49	Evil gal blues	National 9012
NSC50	Salty papa blues	National 9013
NSC51	Albinia's blues	National 9013
NSC52	Don't you wear no black	National 9012
	(What's the matter with me)	

NB Gillespie as "John Kildare" and Price as "Bubber Prince".

1945
July 30   New York

Mezzrow–Bechet Septet
Hot Lips Page (t, v); Mezz Mezzrow (cl); Sidney Bechet (ss); Sammy Price (p); Danny Barker (g); Pops Foster (db); Sid Catlett (d)

KJ12-1	House party		King Jazz 143
KJ12-2	House party		*Storyville (D) SLP137*
KJ13-1	Perdido Street stomp	(EP)	*Storyville (D) SEP411*
KJ13-2	Perdido Street stomp		*Storyville (D) SLP141*
KJ14-1	Revolutionary blues, Part 1		*Storyville (D) SLP153*
KJ15-1	Revolutionary blues, Part 2		*Storyville (D) SLP153*
KJ16-1	Blood on the moon (HLP, v)		King Jazz 143

NB Revolutionary blues also issued as Chicago function and as Old school. Page as "Pappa Snow White" and Price as "Jimmy Blythe Jr".

1945
July 31   New York

Mezzrow–Bechet Septet
Hot Lips Page (t); Mezz Mezzrow (cl); Sidney Bechet (ss); Sammy Price (as "Jimmy Blythe Jr") (p); Danny Barker (g); Pops Foster (db); Sid Catlett (d); Pleasant Joe (Joe Pleasants) (v)

KJ17-1	Levee blues (PJ, v)		King Jazz 144
KJ18-1	Layin' my rules in blues (PJ, v)		*Storyville (D) SLP153*
KJ19-1	Bad, bad baby blues (PJ, v)		*Storyville (D) SLP141*
KJ19-2	Bad, bad baby blues (PJ, v)	(EP)	Storyville (D) SEP411
KJ20-1	Saw mill man blues (PJ, v)		King Jazz 144
KJ21-1	Minor swoon		*Storyville (D) SLP821*
KJ21-2	Minor swoon		*Storyville (D) SLP142*

KJ21-3	Minor swoon	(EP)	Storyville (D) SEP409
KJ22-1	The sheik of Araby	(EP)	Storyville (D) SEP408
KJ22-2	The sheik of Araby		*Storyville (D) SLP153*

Sammy Price (p), with Sid Catlett (d)

KJ23-1	Boogin' with Big Sid	(45)	Dudan (S2) 204

1946
January 11   New York

Sister Rosetta Tharpe (v,g) with the Sam Price Trio
Sammy Price (p); Billy Taylor (db); Wallace Bishop (d)

73274-A	Don't take everybody to be your friend	Decca 11002
73275	Tell the world to sing	Unissued
73276-A	How far from God	Decca 48030
73277-A	When I move to the sky	Decca 11002

1946
May 2   New York

Sister Rosetta Tharpe (v,g) with the Sam Price Trio
Sammy Price (p); Benny Moten (db); Eddie Bourne (d)

73548-A	Jesus is here today	Decca 48013
73549-A	Jonah	Decca 48013
73550	God's mighty hand	*MCA (F) 510.148*
73551	The Lord followed me	Decca 48030

1946
November 9   New York

"Really The Blues" Concert
Muggsy Spanier (c); Sandy Williams (tb); Sidney Bechet (ss); Sammy Price (p); Wellman Braud (db); Baby Dodds (d); Mezz Mezzrow (an)

	Darktown strutters ball	*Jazz Archives JA-39*
	The blues	*Jazz Archives JA-39*
	Muskrat ramble	*Jazz Archives JA-39*

Sammy Price (p); Baby Dodds (d)
> Sammy's boogie woogie blues   *Jazz Archives JA-39*

NB Art Hodes replaced Price for other items from the concert and LP.

1947
July 1   New York

Sister Rosetta Tharpe (v,g) with the Sam Price Trio
Sammy Price (p); Pops Foster (db); Kenny Clarke (d)

73987-A	This train	Decca 48043

Sister Rosetta Tharpe (v,g) and Marie Knight (v) with the Sam Price Trio
Same personnel

73988-A	Oh, when I come to the end of my journey	Decca 48043
73989-A	Didn't it rain	Decca 48054
73990-A	Stretch out	Decca 48054

1947
cJuly   New York

Sister Rosetta Tharpe (v,g) and Marie Knight (v), with Sammy Price (p); Pops Foster (db); Kenny Clarke (d)

DB104A	This train (SRT, v)	Down Beat 104
DB104B	When I come to the end of my journey (SRT & MK, v)	Down Beat 104

NB The artist credit on Down Beat 104 is "Sister Katy Marie".

1947
July 16   New York

Monette Moore (v) with Sam Price and his Trio
Sammy Price (p); Danny Barker (g); Pops Foster (db); Kenny Clarke (d)

74006-A	Another woman's man	Decca 48047
74007-A	Please Mr Blues	Decca 48047

Cousin Joe (Joe Pleasants) (v) with Sam Price and his Trio
Same personnel

| 74008 | Bad luck blues | Decca 48045 |
| 74009 | Box Car Shorty (and Peter Blue) | Decca 48045 |

1947
August 29   New York

Albinia Jones (v) with Sam Price and his Trio

Sammy Price (p); Billy Butler (g); Percy Joell (db); Dorothea Smith (d)

74027	Give it up daddy blues	Decca 48069
74028	The rain is falling	Unissued-rejected
74029	Papa tree top blues	Decca 48048

1947
November 19   New York

Cousin Joe (Joe Pleasants) (v) with Sam Price and his Trio

Sammy Price (p); Billy Butler (g); Percy Joell (db); Dorothea Smith (d)

74142	Beggin' woman	Decca 48091
74143	Sadie Brown	Decca 48061
74144	Evolution blues	Decca 48061
74145	Box Car Shorty's confession	Decca 48091

1947
November 24   New York

Sister Rosetta Tharpe (v,g) and Marie Knight (v) with the Sam Price Trio

Sammy Price (p); Pops Foster (db); Wallace Bishop (d)

74153-A	Beams of heaven	Decca 48070
74154-A	Up above my head I hear music in the air	Decca 48090
74155-A	My journey to the sky	Decca 48090

1947
November 25   New York

Marie Knight (v) with the Sam Price Trio
Sammy Price (p); Pops Foster (db); Wallace Bishop (d)

74160-A	What could I do	Decca 48072
74161-A	I must see Jesus	Decca 48072
74162-A	The land beyond the river	Decca 48084
74163-A	My heavenly Father watches over me	Decca 48084

1947
November 26   New York

Sister Rosetta Tharpe (v,g) with the Sam Price Trio
Sammy Price (p); Pops Foster (db); Wallace Bishop (d)

74166-A	Teach me to be right	Decca 48083
74167-A	I heard my mother call my name	Decca 48166
74168-A	Heaven is not my home	Decca 48190
74169-A	The natural facts	Decca 48166
74170-A	Cain't no grave hold my body down	Decca 48154
74171-A	Lay down your soul	Decca 48083
74173-A	Family prayer	Decca 48190

Sister Rosetta Tharpe (v,g) and Marie Knight (v) with the Sam Price Trio
Same personnel

| 74172-A | Precious memories | Decca 48070 |

1947
November 28   New York

Albinia Jones (v) with Sam Price and his Quartet
Sammy Price (p) unknown (ts, g, db, d)

74184-A	The rain is falling	Decca 48048
74185-A	Love is such a mystery	Decca 48095
74186-A	I have a way of lovin'	Decca 48069
74187-A	Hey little boy	Decca 48095

1947
December 18   Chicago

Mezzrow–Bechet Quintet

Mezz Mezzrow (cl); Sidney Bechet (ss); Sammy Price (as "Jimmy Blythe Jr") (p); Pops Foster (db); Kaiser Marshall (d)

KJ43-1	Where am I		*Storyville (D) SLP137*
KJ43-2	Where am I	(EP)	Storyville (D) SEP411
KJ43-3	Where am I	(12" 78)	King Jazz (E) 3
KJ44-1	Tommy's blues	(12" 78)	King Jazz (E) 7
KJ44-2	Tommy's blues	(EP)	Storyville (D) SEP409
KJ45-1	Chicago function, Part 1	(12" 78)	King Jazz (E) 5
KJ45-2	Chicago function, Part 1		*Storyville (D) SLP141*
KJ46-1	Chicago function, Part 2	(12" 78)	King Jazz (E) 5
KJ46-2	Chicago function, Part 2		*Storyville (D) SLP141*

NB Chicago function also issued as Revolutionary blues.

1947
December 19   Chicago

Mezzrow–Bechet Quintet

Mezz Mezzrow (cl); Sidney Bechet (ss); Sammy Price (as "Jimmy Blythe Jr") (p); Pops Foster (db); Kaiser Marshall (d)

KJ47-1	I want some		King Jazz (E) 8
KJ47-2	I want some		*Storyville (D) SLP142*
KJ48-1	I'm speaking my mind	(EP)	Storyville (D) SEP408
KJ48-2	I'm speaking my mind	(45)	Storyville (D) A45060
KJ48-3	I'm speaking my mind		King Jazz (E) 8
KJ49-1	Never will I forget the blues	(45)	Storyville (D) A45082
KJ49-2	Never will I forget the blues	(45)	King Jazz (I) 201
KJ50-1	The blues and Freud, Part 1		*Storyville (D) SLP136*
KJ51-1	The blues and Freud, Part 2		*Storyville (D) SLP136*
KJ52-1	Kaiser's last break	(EP)	Storyville (D) SEP411
KJ52-2	Kaiser's last break	(12" 78)	King Jazz (E) 11

NB Never will I forget the blues also issued as I ain't gonna do it blues.

1947
December 20   Chicago

Mezzrow–Bechet Quintet

Mezz Mezzrow (cl); Sidney Bechet (ss); Sammy Price (as "Jimmy Blythe Jr") (p); Pops Foster (db); Kaiser Marshall (d)

KJ53-1	I'm goin' away from here	(EP)	Storyville (D) SEP408
KJ53-2	I'm goin' away from here		King Jazz (E) 7
KJ54-1	Funky butt (I got you some)		*Storyville (D) SLP153*
KJ54-2	Funky butt (I must have my boogie)	(EP)	Storyville (D) SEP 394
KJ54-3	Funky butt	(EP)	Storyville (D) SEP403
KJ54-4	Funky butt	(12" 78)	King Jazz (E) 3
KJ55-1	Delta mood		King Jazz (E) 11
KJ55-2	Delta mood	(12)	*Storyville (D) SLP136*
KJ56-1	Blues of the roaring twenties	(45)	King Jazz (I) 204
KJ56-2	Blues of the roaring twenties	(EP)	Storyville (D) SEP402

1947
December 30   New York

Sister Rosetta Tharpe (v, g) with The Dependable Boys (v trio) and the Sam Price Trio

Sammy Price (p); Pops Foster (db); Wallace Bishop (d)

74491-A	Everybody's gonna have a wonderful time up there (Gospel boogie)	Decca 48071
74492-A	My Lord and I	Decca 48071

1948
February   Paris

Sammy Price (p); Georges Hadjo (db); Kenny Clarke (d)

ES23	Eiffel tower	Decca (F) SF159
ES24	Good Paree	Decca (F) SF160
ES25	Low down blues	Decca (F) SF160
ES26	Montparnasse	Decca (F) SF159
ES27	Sammy's boogie	Decca (F) SF161
ES28	Frenchy's blues	Decca (F) SF161

1948
cFebruary   Paris

Sammy Price (p); unknown (wb)–1

Pigalle blues	Whiskey, Women, and	
	(Sw) KM-704	
Eiffel boogie–1	Whiskey, Women, and	
	(Sw) KM-704	

1948
August 20   New York

Clyde Bernhardt (v), with Albert Nicholas (cl); George James (as); John Hardee (ts); Sammy Price (p); ? Williams (g); Walter Williams (db)

74592	Pretty mama blues	Decca 48087
74593	My heart belongs to you	Decca 48087
	Roberta	Decca-unissued
	That's Lulu	Decca-unissued

1948
December 2   New York

Sister Rosetta Tharpe (v, g) and Marie Knight (v) with the Sam Price Trio

Sammy Price (p); Billy Taylor (db); Herbert Cowans (d)–1

74637-A	He watches me–1	Decca 48098
74638-A	He's all I need	Decca 48098

Marie Knight (v) with The Dependable Boys (v trio) and the Sam Price Trio
Same personnel

74640	Gospel train	Decca 48092

Marie Knight (v) with the Sam Price Trio
Same personnel

74639-A	The Florida storm	Decca 48189

Sister Rosetta Tharpe (v, g) with The Dependable Boys and the Sam Price Trio
Same personnel

74641	Down by the riverside	Decca 48106
74642	Little boy	Unissued
74643	My Lord's gonna move this wicked race–1	Decca 48106

1948
December 3   New York

Marie Knight (v) with the Sam Price Trio

Sammy Price (p); Billy Taylor (db); Herbert Cowans (d)

| 74644-A | Hallelujah, what a song | Decca 48189 |
| 74645 | Behold his face | Decca 48092 |

Sister Rosetta Tharpe (v, g) with the Sam Price Trio
Same personnel

| 74646-A | Ain't no room in church for liars | Decca 48154 |

Sister Rosetta Tharpe (v, g) with The Dependable Boys and the Sam Price Trio
Same personnel

74647	Cleanse me	Unissued
74648-A	Little boy 'how old are you'	Decca 48177
74649-A	Going back to Jesus	Decca 48177

1949
January 11   New York

Sister Rosetta Tharpe (v, g) with the Sam Price Trio

Sammy Price (o); Marie Knight (p); Walter Page (db); Kansas Fields (d)

| 74676-A | Move on up a little higher, Part 1 | Decca 48093 |
| 74677-A | Move on up a little higher, Part 2 | Decca 48093 |

1949
February 2   New York

Ethel Davenport (v) with the Jimmy Blythe Jr Trio

Sammy Price (p); possibly Brownie McGhee (g); unknown (db, d)

74741	Hallelujah	Coral 65012
74742	All the way	Coral 65012
74743	Love is like a river	Coral 65005
74744	Each day	Coral 65005

1949
February 11   New York

Albinia Jones (v) with Sam Price and his Rockin' Rhythm

Sammy Price (p); unknown (t, ts, 2 sax, db, d)

74755-A	Song man	Decca 48100
74756	Daddy how you satisfy	Unissued
74757-A	Hole in the wall	Decca 48100

NB Decca 48100 as "Albennie Jones"

1949
March 31   New York

Marie Knight (v) with the Sammy Price Quartet

Sammy Price (p); Ray Ross (o); Brownie McGhee (g); Kansas Fields (d)

74815-A	I can't forget it, can you	Decca 48102
74816-A	Up in my heavenly home	Decca 48102

1949
May 20   New York

Herman "Peetie Wheatstraw" Ray (v), with J.T. Brown (ts);
Sammy Price (p); Lonnie Johnson (g); unknown (db, d)

74935-A	Working man	Decca 48107
79436-A	Trouble blues	Decca 48105
74937-A	President's blues	Decca 48107
74938-A	I'm a little piece of leather	Decca 48105

1949
July 7   New York

Sister Rosetta Tharpe (v, g) and Katie Bell Nubin (v) with the Sam Price Trio

Sammy Price (p); Billy Taylor (db); Herbert Cowans (d)

75038-A	Ninety-nine and a half won't do	Decca 48116
75039-A	Daniel in the lion's den	Decca 48116
75040	The Devil is trying to steal my joy	Unissued
75041	Just look	Unissued

Sam Price and his Rockin' Rhythms
Buck Clayton (t); Vincent Bair-Bey (as, bs); Buddy Tate (ts); Sammy Price (p); Billy Taylor (db); Sid Catlett (d); Jesse Perry (v)

75046	Ain't nobody's business (JP, v)	Vocalion 55023
75047	In the middle of the night (JP, v)	Unissued
75048	Back street	Vocalion 55023
75049	Hold me baby (JP, v)	Unissued

1949
July 8   New York

Marie Knight (v) with the Sammy Price Quartet
Sammy Price (p); Brownie McGhee (g); Billy Taylor (db); Herbert Cowans (d)

75050-A	I thank you Jesus	Decca 48120
75051-A	I must have Jesus all the way	Decca 48120

Marie Knight (v) and Vivian Cooper (v) with the Sammy Price Quartet
Same personnel

75052-A	Out of the depths	Decca 48111
75053-A	Touch me Lord Jesus	Decca 48111

1949
August 6   Eddie Condon's Floor Show   TV Broadcast, New York

Sidney Bechet Quartet

Sidney Bechet (ss); "Big Chief" Russell Moore (tb); Sammy Price (p); Kansas Fields (d)

| Buddy Bolden stomp | *Queen-Disc (I) 029* |

1949
September 2   New York

Ethel Davenport (v) with Jimmy Blythe Jr and his Trio
Sammy Price (p); Al Casey (g); Ernest Hill (db); Herbert Cowans (d)

75223-A	Leaning on the Lord	Coral 65024
75224-A	I will wait till my change comes	Coral 65024
75225	Only a look	Coral 65017
75226	Dig a little deeper in God's love	Coral 65017

1949
November 30   New York

Marie Knight (v) and Alfred Miller (v) with the Sam Price Trio
Sammy Price (p); Billy Taylor (db); Herbert Cowans (d)

| 75550 | Jesus loves me | Decca 48128 |
| 75551 | Whispering hope | Decca 48128 |

Marie Knight (v) and Vivian Cooper (v) with the Sam Price Trio
Same personnel

| 75552 | Jonah and the storm | *MCA MCA-28122* |
| 75553 | In the garden | *MCA MCA-28122* |

Vivian Cooper (v) with the Sam Price Trio
Same personnel

| 75554-A | You can't hurry God | Decca 48134 |
| 75555-A | My home over there (add Alfred Miller, o) | Decca 48134 |

Marie Knight (v) with the Sam Price Quartet
Alfred Miller (o); Sammy Price (p); Billy Taylor (db); Herbert Cowans (d)

| 75556 | Live the life | Decca 48147 |
| 75557 | Seal of heaven | Decca 48147 |

1950

January 31   New York

Professor Johnson (v, g) and his Gospel Singers (v group) with the Sammy Price Trio

Sammy Price (p); unknown (db, d)

75780-A	Where shall I be	Decca 48143
75781-A	Give me that old time religion	Decca 48204
75782-A	Angels	Decca 48143
75783-A	Standing in the safety zone	Decca 48204
	(omit v group)	

1950

November 29   New York

"Scat Man" Bailey (v), with Buddy Tate's Band

Emmett Berry (t); Dickie Wells (tb); Buddy Tate (ts); Dave McRae (bs); Sammy Price (p); Al Morris (g); Walter Page (db); Walter Johnson (d)

F-104	My oh my	Federal 12003
F-105	Raindrop blues	Federal 12003
F-106	Ride soldier ride	Unissued
F-107	Skinny leg woman	Unissued

1951

January 11   New York

Sister Rosetta Tharpe (v, g) with the Sam Price Trio

Sammy Price (p); Walter Page (db); Herbert Cowans (d)

80324	Use me Lord	Decca 48269
80325	Somebody needs Jesus	*MCA MCA-28122*
80326-A	Sin is to blame	Decca 48230
80327-A	I thank God for my song	Decca 48230

1951

late January   New York

The Guiding Light Gospel Singers (female v group) with the Jimmy Blythe Jr Quartet

Sammy Price (p); others unknown

80451	Steal away	Coral 65049
80452	I've got the Holy Ghost	Coral 65055
80453	Just like Jesus did	Coral 65055
80454	Just a closer walk with thee	Coral 65049

1951
February 13   New York

Myrtle Jackson (v) with the Jimmie Blythe Jr Orchestra

Sammy Price (p); Ellsworth Perkins (g); Sylvester Hickman (db); Sid Catlett (d)

80507	Yield not to temptation	Coral 65053
80508	Where can I go	Coral 65053
80509	We'll understand it better	Coral 65081
80510	I call Him Jesus my rock	Coral 65081

1951
February 20   New York

Sister Rosetta Tharpe (v); with the Rosette Gospel Singers (female v group) and the Sam Price Trio

Larry Johnson (o); Sammy Price (p); Abie Baker (db); Herbert Cowans (d)

80587	Throw out the life-line	Decca 14578
80588	Blessed assurance	Decca 14575
80589	Rock of ages	Decca 14576
80590	In the garden	Decca 14577

1951
February 21   New York

Sister Rosetta Tharpe (v); with the Rosette Gospel singers (female v group) and the Sam Price Trio

Larry Johnson (o); Sammy Price (p); Abie Baker (db); Herbert Cowans (d)

80593	Let the lower lights be burning	Decca 14576
80594	There's a fountain filled with blood	Decca 14577
80595	What a friend we have in Jesus	Decca 14578
80596	Amazing grace (add Lottie Henry, v)	Decca 14575

Sister Rosetta Tharpe (v, g) and Marie Knight (v) with the Sam Price Trio

Sammy Price (p); Abie Baker (db); Herbert Cowans (d)

80597-A	I want Jesus to walk around my bedside (before I die)	Decca 48209
80598-A	Royal telephone	Decca 48209
80599-A	Milky white way	Decca 48227
80600-A	His eye is on the sparrow	Decca 48227

1954
August 4   New York

Sister Rosetta Tharpe (v, g) with the Sam Price Trio

Sammy Price (p); Everett Barksdale (g); Hayes Alvis (db); Terry Snyder (d)

86626	Go ahead	Decca 29255
86627	He is everything to me	Decca 48337
86628	Everytime I feel the spirit	Decca 48337

Sister Rosetta Tharpe (v) and Marie Knight (v) with the Sam Price Trio

Same personnel

86629	Look away in the heavenly land	Decca 48332

Sister Rosetta Tharpe (v) with the Sy Oliver Singers (v group)

Marlowe Morris (o); Sammy Price (p); Myor Rosen (harp); Everett Barksdale (g); Hayes Alvis (db); Terry Snyder (d, chimes–1)

86631	When was Jesus born	Decca 48328
86632	In Bethlehem–1	Decca 48328
86633	This ole house	Decca 29255

1954
August 5   New York

Marie Knight (v) with the Sam Price Trio

Sammy Price (p); Everett Barksdale (g); Hayes Alvis (db); Terry Snyder (d)

86635	I'm troubled	Decca 48326
86636	Unknown title	Unissued
86637	Stop now, it's praying time	Decca 48326
86638	Trouble in mind	Decca 48327

1954
December 1   New York

Jimmy Rushing's All Stars

Jimmy Rushing (v); Pat Jenkins (t); Henderson Chambers (tb); Ben Richardson (cl, as); Buddy Tate (ts); Sammy Price (p); Walter Page (db); Jo Jones (d)

> How long, how long   (10″ LP) Vanguard VRS8011
> blues
> Boogie woogie (I may be
> wrong)
> How you want your lovin'
> done?
> Goin' to Chicago blues
> I want a little girl
> Leave me
> Sent for you yesterday

1954
December 6   New York

Marie Knight (v) with the Sam Price Trio

Sammy Price (p); Grady Martin (g); unknown (db); Panama Francis (d)

87147	A traveller's tune	Decca 48334
87148	The battle of Jericho	Decca 48334
87149	The storm is passing over (plus band, v)	Decca 48336
87150	I must tell Jesus	Decca 48336
87151	Who rolled the stone away	Decca 48333
87152	Easter bells	Decca 48333

1955
March 20   New York

Sam Price and his Kaycee Stompers

Jonah Jones (t); Vic Dickenson (tb); Pete Brown (as); Sammy Price (p); Milt Hinton (db); Cozy Cole (d)

> Jumpin' on 57th   *Jazztone J1207*
> Pete's delta bound   *Jazztone J1207*

Jonah whales again (Jonah whales the blues)	*Jazztone J1207*
Manhattan blues (omit Brown)	*Jazztone J1207*

Vic Dickenson (tb); Sammy Price (p, v); Milt Hinton (db); Cozy Cole (d)

Shakin' and rattlin'	(10″ LP)	Jazztone J1008
Sam's pretty blues (SP, v)		*Jazztone J1207*
Rockin' the rocket		Jazztone J1008
If I could be with you (One hour)		*Jazztone J1207*
Stormy weather		*Jazztone J1207*
Walkin' and shoutin' the boogie		*Jazztone J1207*
Please don't talk about me when I'm gone (SP, v)		*Jazztone J1207*

1955
New York

Omer Simeon Trio

Omer Simeon (cl); Sammy Price (p, v); Zutty Singleton (d)

Grand boubousse	(10″ LP) Jazztone J1014
Qua-ti rhythm	
Qua-ti blues	
Lagniappe	
Frankie and Johnny	
Bill Bailey, won't you please come home	
St James infirmary (SP, v)	
Aunt Hager's children	

1955
December 20   Paris

Sammy Price and his Blusicians

Emmett Berry (t); George Stevenson (tb); Herbie Hall (cl); Sammy Price (p); Pops Foster (db); Fred Moore (d)

Swingin' in Paris style	*Jazz Selection (F) LDM30.023*
Paris lament	
USA romp	
Louisiana lament	

	Big mouth Steve from Baltimore	
mst	Blue Berry	
alt	Blue Berry	*Jazz Legacy (F) 500103*
mst	Janine boogie	*Jazz Selection (F) LDM30.023*
alt	Janine boogie	*Jazz Legacy (F) 500103*
mst	Swingin' at Gaveau	*Jazz Selection (F) LDM30.023*
alt	Swingin' at Gaveau	*Jazz Legacy (F) 500103*

1956
January 6   Paris

Emmett Berry and his Orchestra

Emmett Berry (t); Guy Lafitte (ts); Sammy Price (p); Pops Foster (db); Fred Moore (d)

Boogie woogie à la   (10″ LP)   Columbia (F) FP1076
   Parisienne
Sammy plays the blues for
   Mezz
Swingin' the Berry's
I'm wonderin'

1956
January 28   Paris

Sammy Price and his Blusicians

Emmett Berry (t); George Stevenson (tb); Herbie Hall (cl); Sammy Price (p); Pops Foster (db); Fred Moore (d, v)

Swing that rhythm   (10″ LP)   Club Francais Du Disque
                                    (F) J63
New shoes blues (Blues des
   chaussures neuves) (FM, v)
Swingin' Kansas City style
Clarinet créole

Sammy Price (p, v); Pops Foster (db); Fred Moore (d)

Gotta boogie, gotta woogie
   (SP, comments)
Helene's blues (SP, v)

1956

February 21 & 22   Concerts, Fontainebleau, near Paris

Sammy Price and his Blusicians

Emmett Berry (t, v); George Stevenson (tb); Herbie Hall (cl);
Sammy Price (p, v, an); Pops Foster (db); Fred Moore (d, v, wb-1)

Squeeze me	*Jazztone J1260*
Basin Street blues	
The world is waiting for the sunrise	
New Orleans drag	
St James infirmary (EB, v)	
Muskrat ramble	
Trombone blues	
High society	
Jammin' in the cellar	*Jazztone J1236*
Shorty needs a mademoiselle	
My lonesome heart	
New shoes blues (FM, v)	
Fontainebleau boogie	
That's a plenty	
Tiger rag-1	
Royal garden blues	
Boogie A-bomb	
When the saints go marchin' home (SP & band, v)	
Boogie for Pops	Unissued
Drum sticks	Unissued
Fred's basement boogie	Unissued
J.M.F. blues	Unissued
Mountain boogie	Unissued

Sammy Price (p); Pops Foster (db); Fred Moore (d)

Mood (Sammy's mood)	*Jazztone J1260*
My blues	*Jazztone J1260*
Shorty gets a mademoiselle	Unissued
Nancy	Unissued
Pettin' around	Unissued
The blues for Sharon	Unissued
French rhythm	Unissued
Fontainebleau blues	Unissued

1956
February 22   Paris

Sammy Price (p)

Twelve o'clock blues	(EP)	Columbia (F) ESDF1098
Sad blues		Columbia (F) ESDF1098
Jelly roll junior blues		Columbia (F) ESDF1098
D'accord mon Pote boogie		Columbia (F) ESDF1098

1956
April 9   Paris

Sammy Price (p)

Rosetta   *Club Francais Du Disque (F) 72*
I can't give you anything but
  love
Can't help loving that man
Keepin' out of mischief now
Someone to watch over me
Ain't misbehavin'
Baby, won't you please come
  home
Blues in my heart
St Louis blues
Tata's blues
Tea for two
Pinetop's boogie woogie
Willow weep for me
Cinema's boogie (Cinéma)
On the sunny side of the
  street
Valetta
Adieu

1956
May 14   Paris

Sammy Price Trio

Sammy Price (p); Pierre Michelot (db); André "Mac Kac" Reilles (d)

Hot Club boogie   (EP) Ducretet-Thompson (F)
                                46OV244

USIS blues	Ducretet-Thomspon (F) 460V244
Love for sale	(EP) Ducretet-Thompson (F) 460V253

Add Maxime Saury (cl)

The sheik of Araby	Ducretet-Thompson (F) 460V253
Avalon	Ducretet-Thompson (F) 460V253

Add Emmett Berry (t) and Maxime Saury (cl)

Goodbye Paris	Ducretet-Thompson (F) 460V243
Mister New Orleans blues	Ducretet-Thompson (F) 460V243

1956
May 16   Paris

Sidney Bechet with Sammy Price and his Blusicians

Emmett Berry (t); George Stevenson (tb); Herbie Hall (cl); Sidney Bechet (ss); Sammy Price (p); Pops Foster (db); Fred Moore (d)

V5856	St Louis blues	*Swing (F) LDM30.041*
V5857	Tin roof blues	
V5858	Darktown strutters ball	
V5859	Jazz me blues	
V5860	Memphis blues	
V5861	Dinah	
V5862	Yes, we have no bananas today	
V5863	Back home	

1956
October 4   Hackensack, New Jersey

Nappy Brown (v) with the Zippers Quartet (v group) and Kelly Owens Orchestra

Sammy Price (p); unknown (saxes, g, db, d)

SNB6889	I'm getting lonesome	Savoy 1506
SNB6890	I cried like a baby	Savoy 1547
SNB6891	Bye bye baby	Savoy 1514

SNB6892   Little by little (omit the   Savoy 1506
                     Zippers Quartet)

1956
October 17   Hackensack, New Jersey
Sam Price and his Texas Blusicians
King Curtis (ts); Sammy Price (p); Mickey Baker (g); Leonard Gaskin (db); Bobby Donaldson (d)

SSP6893(mst)	Rib joint	Savoy 1505
SSP6893(alt)	Rib joint	*Savoy SJL2240*
SSP6894	After hours swing	*Savoy MG14004*
SSP6895	Tishomingo	Savoy 1505
SSP6896	Back room rock	*Savoy MG14004*

1956
November 21   Hackensack, New Jersey
Sammy Price Sextet
King Curtis (ts); Haywood Henry (bs); Sammy Price (p); Mickey Baker (g); Leonard Gaskin (db); Bobby Donaldson (d)

SSP6908	Bar-B-Q sauce	*Savoy MG14004*
SSP6909	High Price	Unissued
SSP6910	Juke joint	*Savoy MG14004*
SSP6911	Ain't no strain	*Savoy MG14004*

1957
January 24   Hackensack, New Jersey
Sammy Price Sextet
King Curtis (ts); Haywood Henry (bs); Sammy Price (p); Kenny Burrell (g); Jimmy Lewis (db); Bobby Donaldson (d); Alma Simmons (v)

SSP6957	Rock my soul	*Savoy MG14004*
SSP6958	Chicken out	*Savoy MG14004*
SSP6959	Jive joint	*Savoy MG14004*
SSP6960	Gulley stomp	*Savoy MG14004*
SSP6961	Give me your smile (AS, v)	Unissued
SSP6962	Love my man (AS, v)	Unissued

1957
July 6   Paris

Sammy Price and his Orchestra
Lucky Thompson (ts); Sammy Price (p, v); Jean-Pierre Sasson (g);
Pierre Michelot (db); Gerard Pochonet (d)

I want a little girl	*Polydor (F) 46103*	
Paris blues		
Up above my head		
Minor blues		
Sweet Georgia Brown		
How long blues		
Lucky T		
Embassy boogie		

1957
July 25   New York

Billy Lamont (v), with Buster Cooper (tb); Bob McCain (ts); Budd
Johnson (bs); Sammy Price (p); Kenny Burrell (g); Leonard Gaskin
(db); Bobby Donaldson (d); A.K. Salim (arr)

SBL70092	Uncle John been goofin'	Unissued
SBL70093	I'm so sorry	Savoy 1522
SBL70094	I got a rock 'n' roll gal	Savoy 1522
SBL70095	Is you is	Unissued

1957
July 26   New York

The Three Playmates (v) with George Barrow (ts); Jerome
Richardson (ts); Budd Johnson (bs); Sammy Price (p); Kenny
Burrell (g); Joe Benjamin (db); Bobby Donaldson (d); Ernie Wilkins
(arr)

SPM70096	Giddy-up-a-ding-dong	Savoy 1523
SPM70097	It must be love	Savoy 1523
SPM70098	Give your love to me	Savoy 1537
SPM70099	(Do-oo, do-oo) I dreamed	Savoy 1537

1958
February 1   Carnegie Hall, New York

Dixieland at Carnegie Hall Concert

Wild Bill Davison (c); Ricky Nelson (tb); Bob Wilber (cl); Sammy Price (p); Al Hall (db); Buzzy Drootin (d)

Riverboat shuffle	*Roulette R23038*

1958
February 14   New York

Chuck Willis (v) with King Curtis (ts); Teddy Charles (vib); Sammy Price (p); A1 Caiola (g); George Barnes (g); Lloyd Trotman (db); Joe Marshall (d); The Cues (v group)

A-2977	You'll be my love	(45)	Atlantic 2005
A-2978	What am I living for		Atlantic 1179
A-2979	Hang up my rock & roll shoes		Atlantic 1179
A-2980	Keep a-driving		Atlantic 2005

1958
July 7   Knokke Jazz Festival, Belgium

Teddy Buckner and Sidney Bechet

Teddy Buckner (t); Vic Dickenson (tb); Sidney Bechet (ss); Sammy Price (p); Arvell Shaw (db); J.C. Heard (d)

St Louis blues	*Swing (F) LDM30.094*
On the sunny side of the street	
I wish I could shimmy like my sister Kate	
I'm coming Virginia	

Albert Nicholas (cl) replaces Sidney Bechet

Basin Street blues	*Swing (F) LDM30.096*
Indiana	

Sammy Price (p); Arvell Shaw (db); J.C. Heard (d)

Blues

1958

July 10   Cannes Jazz Festival, France

Teddy Buckner and Sidney Bechet

Teddy Buckner (t); Vic Dickenson (tb); Sidney Bechet (ss); Sammy Price (p); Arvell Shaw (db); Roy Eldridge (d)

Rosetta	*Swing (F) LDM30.094*
Sweet Georgia Brown	
Once in a while	

Teddy Buckner (t); Vic Dickenson (tb); Albert Nicholas (cl); Michel Attenoux (ss); Sammy Price (p); Arvell Shaw (db); J.C.Heard (d)

Royal garden blues	*Swing (F) LDM30.096*
Muskrat ramble	

Sammy Price (p); Arvell Shaw (db); J.C. Heard (d)

I Heard J.C.

1958

October   Paris

Sammy Price (p)

The man I love	(2-EP set)	Club Francais Du Disque
		(F) 142
Somebody loves me		
'S wonderful		

Doc Cheatham (t) and Sammy Price (p)

Lady be good
I got rhythm
Summertime
Embraceable you
Rhapsody in blue

1959

March 24   Hackensack, New Jersey

Sammy Price and the All Stars

Sammy Price (p, v); Mickey Baker (g); Al Casey (g); Al Lucas (db); Panama Francis (d)

Sammy sings the blues (SP, v)   *World-Wide MG20016*

SSP70531	Roll 'em Sam	
SSP70532	Kansas City boogie woogie stomp	
SSP70533	Boogie cha cha	
SSP70534	New Orleans blues	
SSP70535	Levee	
SSP70536	The saints boogie	
SSP70537	Blue drag	(45) Savoy 1565
SSP70538	Honky tonk caboose	Savoy 1568
SSP70539	Pack up and boogie	*World-Wide MG20016*
SSP70540	Chicken strut	Savoy 1565
SSP70541	Boogie woogie slop	*World-Wide MG20016*
SSP70542	Wee hours	Savoy 1568

1959
July 7   New York

Lafayette Thomas (v, g) with Sammy Price (p); Bucky Pizzarelli (elb); Belton Evans (d)

SLT70601	Blues	Unissued
SLT70602	Texarkana	Unissued
SLT70603	Please come back to me	Savoy 1574
SLT70604	Lafayette's a-comin'	Savoy 1574

1959
September   New York

Arnold Wiley (v) and his Band

Johnny Letman (t); Buster Bailey (cl); George Kelly (ts); Sammy Price (p); Ralph Williams (g); Gene Ramey (db); "Speedy" (d)

A111	I'll be a long time	Ace 111
A112	Square's ain't walking no more	Ace111

1960
January 22   New York

Wilbert Harrison (v, g) with King Curtis (ts); Sammy Price (p); Jimmy Spruill (g); ? Winston (db); unknown (d)

F-1063	C.C. rider	(45) Fury 1031
F-1064	Why did you leave me	Fury 1031

1960
New York

Wilbert Harrison (v, g) with possibly King Curtis (ts); Sammy Price (p); Jimmy Spruill (g); unknown (db, d)

F-1073	Little schoolgirl	(45) Fury 1037

1960
November 4   New York

Henry "Red" Allen Orchestra

Henry "Red" Allen (t, v); Herb Flemming (tb); Buster Bailey (cl); Sammy Price (p); Milt Hinton (db); Sol Hall (d)

26859	How long, how long blues (HRA, v)	Verve MGV1025
26862	Snowy morning blues	
26863	Baby won't you please come home (HRA, v)	
26865	Yellow dog blues	

1961
April 11   New York

Ida Cox (v) with the Coleman Hawkins Quintet

Roy Eldridge (t); Coleman Hawkins (ts); Sammy Price (p); Milt Hinton (db); Jo Jones (d)

260	Hard time blues	Riverside RLP374
261	Wild women don't have the blues	
262	Death letter blues	
263	Blues for Rampart Street	
264	Cherry pickin' blues	

1961
April 12   New York

Ida Cox (v) with the Coleman Hawkins Quintet

Same personnel as 11 April 1961

265	Fogyism	*Riverside RLP374*
266	Mama goes where papa goes	
267	Ida Cox's lawdy lawdy blues	
268	St Louis blues	
269	Hard, oh Lord	

1961
September 15   London House, Chicago

Henry "Red" Allen Quartet
Henry "Red" Allen (t); Sammy Price (p); Frank Skeete (db); Jerry Potter (d)

Algiers bounce (theme)	*Fanfare 24-124*
Lover come back to me	
Do you know what it means to miss New Orleans?	
Tenderly	
Bill Bailey, won't you please come home?	
Rosetta	
All of me	
Algiers bounce (theme)	

1961
September 22   London House, Chicago

Henry "Red" Allen Quartet
Henry "Red" Allen (t); Sammy Price (p); Frank Skeete (db); Jerry Potter (d)

Algiers bounce (theme)	*Fanfare 24-124*
Ballin' the jack	
Snowy morning blues	
Autumn leaves	
Love is just around the corner	
Basin Street blues	
Algiers bounce (theme)	

1961
late September   New York

Sammy Price and his Blusicians with Doc Horse (Al Pittman) (v)

Vic Dickenson (tb)–1; Sammy Price (p); Freddie Green (g); Eddie Jones (db); Sonny Payne (d)

6078	Nobody knows you when you're down and out	*Kapp KLP1267*
6079	Piney Brown blues–1	
6080	Key to the highway–1	

Vic Dickenson (tb); Sammy Price (p); Eddie Jones (db); Sonny Payne (d)

6098	How long, how long blues
6099	Wee baby blues
6100	Trouble in mind
6101	In the dark
6102	Confessin' the blues
6103	I'm gonna move to the outskirts of town
6110	The blues ain't nothin' but a good man feelin' bad

1962
March 23   London House, Chicago

Henry "Red" Allen Quartet
Henry "Red" Allen (t, an); Sammy Price (p); Frank Skeete (db); Jerry Potter (d)

Lover come back to me   *Flutegrove (E) FL6*
St Louis blues
That's a plenty
Medley: I've grown
   accustomed to her face/
   Autumn leaves
Biffly blues
Bill Bailey won't you please
   come home

1962
March 30   London House, Chicago

Henry "Red" Allen Quartet
Henry "Red" Allen (t, an); Sammy Price (p); Frank Skeete (db); Jerry Potter (d)

Aunt Hagar's blues   *Flutegrove (E) FL6*
The Price is right
Medley: It's all right with me/
       Hava Neguila
Jelly roll blues

1962
Summer   New York

Bea Booze (Muriel Nicholls) (v, g) and Sammy Price (p)

| 107 | Good time poppa | (45) | Stardust 107/8 |
| 108 | What else ain't-cha got? | | Stardust 107/8 |

1965
August 18 & 19   Blue Spruce Inn, Roslyn, Long Island

Henry "Red" Allen Quartet

Henry "Red" Allen (t, v, an); Sammy Price (p); Benny Moten (db); George Reed (d)

Blue Spruce boogie	*Merit 27*
Gee baby, ain't I good to you? (HRA, v)	*Columbia 2447*
Caravan	*Merit 27*
You're nobody 'til somebody loves you (HRA, v)	*Columbia 2447*
Sweet substitute (HRA, v)	*Columbia 2447*
Hello Dolly (HRA, v)	*Merit 27*
Feeling good (HRA, v)	*Columbia 2447*
Patrol wagon blues (HRA, v)	*Columbia 2447*
Never on Sunday	*Merit 27*
Medley: Yellow dog blues/ How long blues (HRA, v)	*Columbia 2447*
Crazy blues	*Merit 27*
I'm coming Virginia	*Columbia 2447*
Satin doll	*Merit 27*
Trav'lin' all alone (HRA, v)	*Columbia 2447*
Rag mop (HRA, v)	
Cherry (HRA, v)	
Siesta at the fiesta	
Memphis blues	*Merit 27*

NB The 7 further items from these sessions on *Meritt 27* have Lannie Scott in place of Price.

1969
November 14   Bordeaux, France

Sammy Price (p)

All keys boogie	*Black and Blue (F) 33.025*
Back beat boogie	
Midnight boogie	
Boogie-woogie soul train	
Pinetop's boogie	
In the evening	
Panassie discovered jazz blues	
Goodbye blues	
Lenox Avenue blues	
F-minor blues	
Jeune fille boogie	*Black and Blue (F) 33.040*
Le train est parti boogie	
Out of sight boogie	
Funky butt boogie	
Candy, Nancy and Sharon blues	
Entendu blues	
Josette got the blues	
Aquilina's dilemma blues	
See see rider	

1969
December 4   London

Sammy Price (p, v)

Honey Grove blues	*Black Lion (E) BLP30130*
St James infirmary (SP, v)	*Black Lion (E) BLP30130*
Jelly on my mind	*Black Lion (E) BLP30201*
Blues for the Blusicians	*Black Lion (E) BLP30201*
Boogie woogie minuet	*Black Lion (E) BLP30201*
How long blues (SP, v)	*Black Lion (E) BLP30201*

Keith Smith (t); Roy Williams (tb); Sandy Brown (cl); Sammy Price (p, v); Ruan O'Lochlainn (g); Harvey Weston (db); Lennie Hastings (d)

West End boogie	*Black Lion (E) BLP30130*
Keepin' out of mischief now (SP, v)	*Black Lion (E) BLP30130*
Struttin' with Georgia	*Black Lion (E) BLP30130*

	Royal Garden blues	*Black Lion (E) BLP30201*
	Hungarian rhapsody (omit Smith)	*Black Lion (E) BLP30201*
	Just a lonesome babe in the wood (omit Smith)	*Black Lion (E) BLP30201*
mst	In the evening (omit Smith & Williams)	*Black Lion (E) BLP30130*
alt	In the evening (omit Smith & Williams)	*Black Lion (E) BLP30201*
	Rosetta (omit Williams & Brown)	*Black Lion (E) BLP30130*

1969
Probably London

Sammy Price (p), with John Defferary (cl); Sammy Rimington (as); unknown (db); Dave Evans (d)

C-jam blues	*Dixie Records (E) 12*
Paper moon	
Lover come back to me	

1975
c Spring   Probably New York (from audition discs)

Marie Buggs (v), with Sammy Price (p)

Do your duty	*Whiskey, Women & (Sw) KM-702*
Empty bed blues	
Good old wagon	
Backwater blues	

1975
May 1   Paris

Sammy Price (p), with Doc Cheatham (t); Gene Conners (tb); Ted Buckner (as); Carl Pruitt (db); J.C. Heard (d)

West End boogie	*Black and Blue (F) 33.079*
Whodat blues	
Riffin' boogie	
'T ain't nobody's bizzness	

Sammy Price (p); Carl Pruitt (db); J.C. Heard (d)

> Back home again in France
> Black and blue blues (Tin roof blues)
> Walkin' down Pigalle
> Memories boogie
> Funky
> Boogie-woogie for Hughes
> Salute to Basie

1975
May 2   Paris

Doc Cheatham (t, v), with Gene Conners (tb); Ted Buckner (as);
Sammy Price (p); Carl Pruitt (db); J.C. Heard (d)

> Rosetta   *Black and Blue (F) 33.090*
> Blues in my heart
> What can I say after I say I'm
>   sorry (DC, v)
> St James infirmary
> Sugar
> If I could be with you (One
>   hour) (DC, v)
> Rose room

Doc Cheatham (t); Sammy Price (p)

> I cover the waterfront

1975
May 12   Paris

Sammy Price (p), with Doc Cheatham (t, v); Gene Conners (tb);
Ted Buckner (as); Carl Pruitt (db); J.C. Heard (d); Marie Buggs (v)

> Squeeze me   *Black and Blue (F) 33.560*
> Boogie with riffs
> I want a little girl (DC, v)   *Black and Blue (F) 33.560*
> Cocktail for two
> Last boogie
> Rockin' boogie
> What can I say after I say I'm
>   sorry (DC, v)
> Willow weep for me
> Empty bed blues   (MB, v)
> Backwater blues   (MB, v)

Sammy Price (p); Carl Pruitt (db); J.C. Heard (d)
> In the evening
> Trouble in mind

1975
May 20   Toulouse, France

Sammy Price (p), with Doc Cheatham (t); Gene Connors (tb); Ted Buckner (as); Carl Pruitt (db); J.C. Heard (d)

Ain't she sweet	(CD)	Black and Blue (F) 233.079
Blues for Dr Boute		Black and Blue (F) 233.079

1975
May 21   Toulouse, France

Sammy Price (p), with Doc Cheatham (t); Gene Connors (tb); Ted Buckner (as); Carl Pruitt (db); J.C. Heard (d)

For you my love (?v)	(CD)	Black and Blue (F) 233.079
Muskrat ramble		Black and Blue (F) 233.079

1975
May 25   Paris

Sammy Price (p), with J.C. Heard (d)

My blue heaven	*Black and Blue (F) 33.111*
St James infirmary	
Gee baby, ain't I good to you?	
Sunday	
J.C. speaks	
Can't help lovin' that man	
Stormy weather	
Berne's boogie	
Sammy & J.C.'s boogie	
Barefoot boogie	
Untitled boogie	
Goin' back home boogie	
Cow Cow boogie	

1975
July 22   Antibes, France

Sammy Price (p, v); Arvell Shaw (db); Panama Francis (d)

The king boogie, Part 1	*Mahogany (F) 558.102*
The king boogie, Part 2 (SP, v)	
Making whoopee	
Keeping out of mischief now (SP, v)	
Bass and piano talking	
Please don't talk about me when I'm gone (SP, v)	
My blue heaven	
St James infirmary (SP, v)	
Boogie woogie French style	
Baby, won't you please come home? (SP, v)	
Trouble in mind	

1975
September 1   Copenhagen, Denmark

Sammy Price (p, v), with Fessor's Big City Band

Finn Otto Hansen (t, flh); Ole "Fessor" Lindgreen (tb, v); Elith "Nulle" Nykjaer (cl, as, hca); Steen Vig (ss, ts); Preben Lindhardt (elb, db); Thorkild Møller (d)

Copenhagen boogie	*Storyville (D) SLP266*
Please don't talk about me when I'm gone (SP, v)	
Blue moment (omit Lindgreen & Nykjaer)	
Chicken out	
Copenhagen blues	
Honeysuckle rose	
St Louis blues (OL, v)	

Sammy Price (p)

Begin the beguine

1975
September 2   Copenhagen, Denmark

*Sammy Price (p, v) & Torben "Plys" Petersen (p), with Preben
Lindhardt (db); Thorkild Møller (d)*

The boogie woogie twins	*Storyville (D) SLP278*
No one to love me blues (SP, v)	
Two piano boogie	
Ain't misbehavin'	
Birmingham blues	
Down on the Copenhagen docks	
Playing the blues for Marc	
Stridin' the saints (When the saints go marching in)	
Baby, won't you please come home? (SP, v)	
Moanin' the blues	

1976
November 17   Toronto, Canada

Doc Cheatham (t) and Sammy Price (p)

Honeysuckle rose	*Sackville (C) 3013*
Doc and Sam's blues	
Summertime	
Tishomingo blues	
The sheik of Araby	
I can't give you anything but love	
You can depend on me	
Ain't misbehavin'	
Dear old southland	

1977
New York

Rahsaan Roland Kirk

*Eddie Preston (t); Steve Turre (tb); Jim Buffington (french horn,
arr); Kenneth Harris (flute); Roland Kirk (ts, arr); William S.
Fischer (electric p); Sammy Price (p); Philip Bowler (db); Sonny
Brown (d); strings (7 violins, 3 violas, 3 cellos)*

Boogie woogie string along   *Warner Brothers BSK3085*
    for real

Roland Kirk (ts-1, cl-2, v, arr); Sammy Price (p); Tiny Grimes (g); Arvell Shaw (db); Gifford McDonald (d)

In a mellotone–1
Make me a pallet on the
    floor–2 (RKv)

Roland Kirk (ts–1, hca–2, arr); Sammy Price ("toy" p)

I loves you Porgy–1
Summertime–2

1977
November 2   Paris

Sammy Price (p), with Johnny Letman (t); Freddy Lonzo (tb); George Kelly (ts); Bill Pemberton (db); Ronnie Cole (d)

I'm coming Virginia   *Black and Blue (F) 33.154*
Just right
Basin Street blues
That's boogie
St Louis blues
On the sunny side of the
    street
The wine of the region blues
Beale Street blues

1978
April 28   International Jazz Festival, Bern, Switzerland

Sammy Price and Jay McShann

Sammy Price (p, v); Leonard Gaskin (db); Oliver Jackson (d)

St James infirmary blues (SP, v) *Philips (H) 9198.203*
In the evening
The Price is right

Sammy Price (p); Jay McShann (p); Leonard Gaskin (db); Oliver Jackson (d)

Blues for two pianos
Boogie for Jay and Sam

Sammy Price (p); Jay McShann (p); Piano Red (p, v); Johnny Shines (g, v); Leonard Gaskin (db); Oliver Jackson (d); Carrie Smith (v)

Medley: Everyday I have the
blues/Goin' to Chicago/ Let
it roll   (CS, PR, JS, v)

1978
May 15   Bern, Switzerland

Sammy Price (p); Denis Progin (d)

Jazzland boogie	*Evasion (Sz) EB-100218*
Ox-tail blues	
Ivory coast blues	
Play the blues for J.J.	
Memory of the Schweizerhof Hotel in Bern (Blue Monk)	
Go Denis go	
The Swiss boogie	
Sako-Anoh bush boogie (Tin roof blues)	
Yesterday	
Walkin' down the Champs Elysees	
Valetta's dream	

*c*1979
West Germany

Sammy Price (p), with Ragtime Specht Groove

Probably: Hans-Jurgen Bock (p); Klaus Schulze (db); Elmar Wippler (d)

West End boogie   *Intercord (G) 155002*

*c*1979
USA

Natalie Lamb (v); Doc Cheatham (t); Sammy Price (p); Candy McDonald (d)

My daddy rocks me   *GHB GHB-84*
Backwater blues
Gimme a pigfoot
Make me a pallet on the floor
'T ain't nobody's business if I
  do
I need a little sugar
Oh papa
Jazzin' baby blues
Frosty mornin' blues
St Louis blues

1979
October 31   Toronto, Canada

Doc Cheatham (t) & Sammy Price (p)

Travelin' all alone   *Sackville (C) 3029*
Some of these days
Love will find a way
After you've gone
Someday you'll be sorry
Old fashioned love
I'm coming Virginia
Squeeze me
Memphis blues
I've got a feeling I'm falling
Louisiana

1979
November 1   Toronto, Canada

Sammy Price (p)

It don't mean a thing   *Sackville (C) 3024*
A hundred years from today
Toronto at midnight
Am I blue?
Aunt Hagar's blues
Don't blame me
Sweet substitute
My lonesome heart
Snowy morning blues

> Medley: Memories of you/As
> time goes by/Misty
> Stormy weather
> McClear Place boogie

1982
April   Melbourne, Australia

Sammy Price (p, v), with Geoff Bull (t, v); Orange Kellin (cl); Lars Edegran (g)

	Back of the bus boogie	(Cassette)	Anteater (Au) 010
	Just a gigolo (GB, v)		
	Back home (in Indiana)		
Take 1	New Orleans		
Take 3	New Orleans		
	Shake that thing (SP, v)		
	Poor butterfly		
	'T ain't nobody's business if I do (SP, v)		

Sammy Price (p, v), with Lars Edegran (g)

> Down under blues (SP, v)

Sammy Price (p)

> Sam's boogie

1983
June 15   Boston

Sammy Price (p, v)

	After hours at the Copley Bar	*Whiskey, Women & (Sw)* KM-702
	Room 509 (SP, v)	
	Trouble in mind (SP, v)	
	509 boogie	
	Box Car Shorty's return (SP, v)	
	Back Bay bounce	
	Ain't nobody's business if I do (SP, v)	
	Bean town boogie	
	Movin' that thing (SP, v)	

1987   New York

Sammy Price (p, v); Ronnie Cole (d)-1

Big Bubba boogie-1   (cassette) Sammy Price Records,
                                   Volume 1

Western boogie-1
Straight ahead boogie-1
Changing keys boogie-1
Shakin' that thing-1 (SP, v)
When the Saints go marchin'-1
    (SP, v)
Long gone boogie-1
Get with it boogie-1
Goin' down slow boogie
The lonesome boogie
Slow drag boogie
Sit down brother-1 (SP, v)
Up above my head-1 (SP, v)
Long gone boogie-1
Boogie woogie rocket
Sammy's boogie-1
unknown title-1

16 unknown titles   (cassette) Sammy Price Records,
                                  Volume 2

I got the whimp blues (cassette) Sammy Price Records,
                                  Volume 3

Boogie me to sleep
Royal Garden blues-1

Take 1   I can't give you anything but
            love-1 (SP, v)

Take 2   I can't give you anything but
            love-1 (SP, v)
          I'm coming Virginia-1
          I hate myself blues (I'm mean
            and evil)-1 (SP, v)
          Ain't misbehavin'-1
          Love me baby as hard as
            you can-1
          How high the moon
          Begin the beguine
          All the things you are
          God bless the child

Blue skies
It don't mean a thing (SP, v)
My baby's gone (SP, v)
unknown title

NB   These three cassettes of private recordings are sold by Sammy at his gigs.

1987
August 10   Houston

Sammy Price (p), with Derrick Lewis (db); Mike Lefebvre (d)

Jazz heritage boogie   (12" LP) *Fantasy F-9659*

1988
April 23   New Orleans

Doc Cheatham (t, v) and Sammy Price (p, v) with Lars Edegran's Jazz Band

Fred Lonzo (tb); Pud Brown (cl, ts); Lars Edegran (g, arr); Frank Fields (db); Ernest Elly (d)

That da-da strain   *GHB GHB-249*
I can't get started
I can't believe that you're in
   love with me
Deed I do
Please don't talk about me
   when I'm gone (SP, v)
Poor butterfly
Sweet Lorraine
G.B. boogie
My blue heaven

SELECTED 12" LPs

LP Label & number	Album title	Price tracks	Session date(s)
Black and Blue (France)			
33.005	Sammy Price: Blues et Boogie Woogie	9	28 Jan & 9 April 1956
33.025	Sammy Price: Midnight Boogie	10	14 Nov 1969
33.040	Sammy Price: Blues & Boogies, vol. 2	9	14 Nov 1969
33.079	Sammy Price:Fire	11	1 May 1975
33.090	Doc Cheatham: Hey Doc!	8	2 May 1975
33.111	Sammy Price: Boogie & Jazz Classics	13	25 May 1975
33.154	Sammy Price: Just Right	8	2 Nov 1977
33.560	Sammy Price: Rockin' Boogie	12	12 May 1975
Black Lion (England)			
BLP30130	Sammy Price: Barrelhouse & Blues	7	4 Dec 1969
BLP30201	Sammy Price: Blues on my Mind	8	4 Dec 1969
Blues Documents (Austria)			
BD–2005	Lee Brown: Piano Blues Rarities, 1937–1940	4	24 March 1939
CBS (England)			
BPG62400	Henry "Red" Allen: Feeling Good	11	18 & 19 Aug 1965
Circle (USA)			
CLP73	Sammy Price & his Blusicians, 1944	21	1 March 1944
Dixie Records (England)			
12	Texas & Louisiana Piano	3	1969
Document (Austria)			
DLP511	Johnnie Temple, 1935–1939	5	6 March & 13 Sept 1939
DLP515	Jimmie Gordon, 1934–1941	9	12 May & 21 Oct 1938, 28 April & 29 Sept 1939, 4 June 1940
Evasion (Switzerland)			
EB100218	Sammy Price: Blues & Boogie Woogie	11	15 May 1978

Everybodys (USA)
EV1002 — Chu Berry, 1937–1940 — 4 — 18 April 1939

Fanfare (USA)
24-124 — Henry "Red" Allen: Live at the London House — 15 — 15 & 22 Sept 1961

Fat Cats Jazz (USA)
FJC-015 — Sidney Bechet & the Blues Singers, vol. 3 — 12 — 26 May 1938

Flutegrove (England)
FL6 — The Great Henry "Red" Allen — 11 — 23 & 30 March 1962

GHB (USA)
GHB-84 — Natalie Lamb – Sammy Price & the Blues — 10 — c1979
GHB-249 — Doc Cheatham/Sammy Price: In New Orleans — 9 — 23 April 1988

Jazz Anthology (France)
JA5211 — Sammy Price: New York, 1955 — 9 — 20 March 1955
JA5192 — Sammy Price: In Europe, 1955 [sic] — 10 — 21 & 22 Feb 1956

Jazz Archives (USA)
JA39 — Sidney Bechet & Mezz Mezzrow: Really the Blues — 4 — 9 Nov 1946
JA46 — Red Allen & the Blues Singers, vol. 1 — 4 — 17 Nov & 13 Dec 1939
JA47 — Red Allen & the Blues Singers, vol. 2 — 7 — 11 Aug & 22 Nov 1938, 17 Nov & 13 Dec 1939

Jazz Legacy (France)
500.103 — Sammy Price: Blues & Boogie — 11 — 20 Dec 1955

Kapp (USA)
KLP1267 — Sammy Price: the Blues Ain't Nothin'. . . — 10 — Sept 1961

Mahogany (France)
558.012 — The New Sammy Price: King of Boogie Woogie — 11 — 22 July 1975

MCA (USA)
1317 — Sister Rosetta Tharpe: Gospel Train — 11 — 1944–48 Decca items
MCA-28122 — Sr R Tharpe & Marie Knight Gospel Keepsakes — 9 — 1949–54 Decca items

Meritt (USA)			
27	Red Allen & his Quartet: Live, 1965	7	18 & 19 Aug 1965
Oldie Blues (Holland)			
OL8008	Cousin Joe From New Orleans: In His Prime	6	16 July & 19 Nov 1947
Pathe (France)			
1552601	Boogie Woogie à la Parisienne	10	6 Jan, 22 Feb & 14 May 1956
Philips (Holland)			
9198.203	Sammy Price & Jay McShann: Blues & Boogie	6	28 April 1978
Polydor (France)			
46103	Sammy Price & his Orchestra	8	6 July 1957
Riverside (USA)			
RLP374	Ida Cox: Blues for Rampart Street	10	11 & 12 April 1961
Sackville (Canada)			
3013	Doc Cheatham & Sammy Price: Doc & Sammy	9	17 Nov 1976
3024	Sammy Price: Sweet Substitute	12	1 Nov 1979
3029	Doc Cheatham & Sammy Price: Black Beauty	11	31 Oct 1979
Savoy (USA)			
SJL2233	Ladies Sing the Blues	4	14 April 1945
SJL2240	Sam Price: Rib Joint: Roots of Rock 'n' Roll (double album)	25	17 Oct & 21 Nov 1956, 24 Jan 1957, 24 March 1959
Storyville (Denmark)			
SLP6004	King Jazz, vol. 1: Out of the Gallion		
SLP6005	King Jazz, vol. 2: Really the Blues		
SLP6006	King Jazz, vol. 3: Gone Away Blues		(Almost) Complete 1945 & 1947 King Jazz sessions
SLP6007	King Jazz, vol. 4: Revolutionary Blues		
SLP4115	King Jazz, vol. 5: I'm Speaking my Mind		
SLP820/821	King Jazz, vols. 7 & 8 (double album)		

SLP226	Sammy Price With Fessor's Big City Band: Copenhagen Boogie	8	1 Sept 1975
SLP278	Sammy Price & Torben "Plys" Petersen	10	2 Sept 1975

Swing (France)

LDM30.094	Festival de Jazz, 1958	7	7 & 10 July 1958
LDM30.096	Jazz Festival	6	7 & 10 July 1958

Swingtime (Italy)

BT2002	Sam Price: Singing With Sammy, vol. 1	14	1938–44 Decca items
ST1029	Sammy Price: Sweepin' the Blues Away, vol. 2	18	1940–45 Decca items

Vanguard (USA)

VRS8518	Jimmy Rushing: Going to Chicago	7	1 Dec 1954

Verve (USA)

MGV 1025	Henry "Red" Allen Plays King Oliver	4	4 Nov 1960

Vogue (England)

VJD552	Sidney Bechet: Refreshing Tracks (double album)	8	16 May 1956

Warner Brothers (USA)

BSK3085	Rahsaan Roland Kirk: Boogie Woogie String Along	5	1977

Whiskey, Women & (Sweden)

KM702	Sam Price: Play It Again Sam	13	cSpring 1975, 15 June 1983
KM704	Sam Price: Do You Dig My Jive	16	Sept 1929, 1948 (Paris) & 1940–42 Decca items

Cassette
Anteater (Australia)

010	Sammy Price: Australia, 1982	10	April 1982

Compact Disc
Black and Blue (France)

CD233079	Sammy Price: Fire	15	1, 20 & 21 May 1975

Index